JUSTIN HALPERN is the founding editor of the comedy website HolyTaco.com and was a senior writer at Maxim.com. In 2009, Halpern created the Twitter page @sh*tmydadsays, which now boasts over three million followers. He co-created and produced a sitcom adaptation for CBS, and has served as a writer on other television series. He splits his time between Los Angeles and San Diego, with his wife Amanda.

Praise for *Sh*t My Dad Says*

'Sam Halpern is an astonishing, forceful, no-nonsense armchair philosopher who, in spite of a great education and a career as an esteemed oncologist, swears like a navvy . . . Funny, silly, honest, lively and fresh'
Sunday Times

'*Sh*t My Dad Says* captures the awkward formative moments between father and son – the hangovers, the first break-up, sex education . . . In many ways Halpern Snr is the voice of reason in a world where we spend too long pussy-footing around, fearful of creating offence'   *Independent*

'You will roar with laughter'   *Sun*

'Ridiculously hilarious'
CHELSEA HANDLER, *New York Times* bestselling author
of *Are you there, Vodka? It's me, Chelsea*

'Justin Halpern tosses lightning bolts of laughter out of his pocket like he is shooting dice in a back alley. In one sweep of a paragraph, he ranges from hysterical to disgusting to touching – and does it all seamlessly. *Sh*t My Dad Says* is a really, really funny book'
LAURIE NOTARO, *New York Times* bestselling author
of *The Idiot Girls' Action-Adventure Club*

Also by Justin Halpern

Sh*t My Dad Says

More Sh*t My Dad Says

Justin Halpern

PAN BOOKS

First published 2012 as *I Suck at Girls* by Macmillan

First published in paperback 2013 as *More Sh*t My Dad* Says by Pan Books
an imprint of Pan Macmillan, a division of Macmillan Publishers Limited
Pan Macmillan, 20 New Wharf Road, London N1 9RR
Basingstoke and Oxford
Associated companies throughout the world
www.panmacmillan.com

ISBN 978-1-4472-3684-9

9 8 7 6 5 4 3 2

A CIP catalogue record for this book is available from
the British Library.

Printed and bound by CPI Group (UK) Ltd, Croydon, CR0 4YY

Visit *www.panmacmillan.com* to read more about all our books
and to buy them. You will also find features, author interviews and
news of any author events, and you can sign up for e-newsletters
so that you're always first to hear about our new releases.

For Amanda

Contents

More
Sh*t
My Dad
Says

You Could Probably Be Happily Married to a Hundred and Fifty Million Different Women

In May 2008, after being dumped by my girlfriend of almost three years, I moved back home with my parents. After patting me on the back and telling me not to "leave my bedroom looking like it was used for a gang bang," my retired seventy-three-year-old father soon started treating me as his full-time conversation partner, the proverbial wall against which he'd fling all his comments to see what stuck.

One day I decided to start chronicling the absurd things that came out of his mouth in a Twitter feed called Shit My Dad Says. What began as an attempt to take my mind off my heartache, and make a couple friends laugh, exploded: within two months I had more than half a million followers, a book deal with a major publisher, and a TV deal, which is all the more ridiculous when you take into account that it was solely because I was just writing down things my dad said. They weren't even my words. To say I was "lucky" would be inaccurate. Finding your wallet after you've left it in a crowded bar is lucky. Getting a book deal and a TV show based on less than five hundred total words is a level of luck reserved for people who survive plane crashes or find out they're Oprah's long-lost sister.

But none of the events of the past year and a half would have occurred if my girlfriend, Amanda, hadn't broken up with me. If she'd never dumped me, I would never have moved home. If I hadn't moved home, I would never have started chronicling the shit my dad says. And if I hadn't started doing that, I would probably still be sitting in the public library next to a homeless man, just as I am right now, but I wouldn't be writing a book. I'd be stealing rolls of toilet paper since I couldn't afford to buy them.

A couple months after I moved home, before I even started the Twitter feed, Amanda called and said she wanted to meet for lunch to talk. It was the first time we'd spoken since the breakup, and I wasn't sure how I felt about seeing her again. We had dated for almost three years, and though calling someone "The One" makes her sound like she was chosen to lead a rebellion against an evil ruler of the galaxy, I genuinely thought Amanda was the person I wanted to spend my life with. It had taken me the two months we hadn't spoken just to start feeling normal again. So the thought of seeing her now was frightening. Seeing someone you used to date is a lot like watching highlights of your favorite team losing in the Super Bowl: just the sight of it hits you like a punch in the gut and makes you remember how upset you were when it all went down in flames.

After I got off the phone with Amanda, I hopped up off the air mattress on my bedroom floor and walked into my dad's office. I told him that Amanda wanted to talk with me and I wasn't sure what to do.

"You're not fucking perfect," he said as he swiveled his chair away from me and back to his desk where he was writing.

"What? I didn't say anything about being perfect. I just wanted to know what you thought," I said, shifting my weight from foot to foot in his doorway.

He swiveled back toward me. "That's what I think. I think you're not perfect."

I explained to him as patiently as I could that I had absolutely no idea what question he was answering, but I was pretty sure it wasn't the one I asked.

"Human beings do dumb shit. You do dumb shit. She does dumb shit. Everyone does dumb shit. Then, every once in a while, we have a moment where we don't do dumb shit, and then we throw a god-damned parade and we forget all the dumb shit we did. So what I'm saying to you is, don't do something, or not do something, to punish someone because you think they did something dumb. Do what you want to do, because it's what you want to do. Also, bring me a grape-fruit from the kitchen and some salt and pepper."

I decided to have lunch with Amanda.

A year later, I sat across from my father in a booth at Pizza Nova, a small restaurant on the San Diego harbor.

"I have big news," I said, barely containing my smile.

"You're in trouble. Is it money? It's money," he said.

"What? No. Why would I say 'I have big news' if it was something bad?"

" 'I have big news; I shot and killed a man.' See, that would be big news to tell someone," he said.

"People don't use that phrase that way," I said.

"Oh, I forgot, you're a writer. You know how everyone in the world fucking talks," he responded.

You can't drive a conversation with my dad. You have to let him drive it, yell directions to him when you can, and hold on until, God willing, you arrive safely at the destination you were hoping to reach. And it's even worse when he's hungry, which he was just then.

"Okay, well, I don't have *bad* big news, then. I have *good* big news," I said, treading more carefully.

"Hit me with it," he said, as he perused the menu.

"I'm going to propose to Amanda," I declared. I had finally said the words out loud to another human being. A giant weight had been lifted off my shoulders.

"Good for you. I think I'm going to get the romaine and watercress salad. I know I always get it, but it's tasty, and what the hell, right?" he said.

My dad's not a real excitable guy, but I'd been hoping for a better response than you'd get by telling someone, "I just won tickets to a Depeche Mode concert." I waited a few more moments, hoping maybe he had something more to add.

"You know what? I should get a pizza," he said, picking the menu back up again.

I fiddled with the straw in my iced tea, trying to figure out how to get back on track. He was the first person I'd told about my plan, and I was determined to get a response that matched how I was feeling.

"So, yep. I'm gonna propose. And then we're going to get married. I'm really excited," I said, staring at the menu in front of his face.

"Good stuff," he said from behind it.

"Dad. I'm telling you I'm getting married. I thought you'd be more excited about this. It's a big deal for me."

My dad pulled the menu down, revealing the same deadpan look he had as he sat through the Ashton Kutcher movie *What Happens in Vegas* after my mother rented it.

"Son, this *is* me excited. I don't know what you want from me. I'm happy for you and Amanda, and I like you both very much, but it's not a surprise. You've been dating her for four years. It ain't like you found a parallel fucking universe," he said before flagging down our waitress, who came over and took our orders.

He was right. It *wasn't* a surprise. And I should have known better anyway. I love my father dearly, but if I was looking for someone to jump up and down with excitement, why did I choose the man who called my sixth-grade graduation "boring as dog shit"?

"I think you have what we in the medical profession call a 'taut sphincter,' " my dad said.

"What?"

"A tight asshole. You're nervous, that's why you're trying to fill dead air with garbage. I'm old and I'm hungry, so cut through the bullshit and just say what you want to say, son," he said.

The day before, I had purchased an engagement ring from a little jewelry shop in La Jolla, California, and up until that moment, I hadn't felt the least bit squeamish about getting married. But then, after I handed my down payment to the eighty-year-old behind the counter and had the ring in my hand, a memory came to me: I was nine years old and crouching in the corner of the bathroom with my pants around my ankles, trying to pee into a water balloon. The idea was to throw the pee-filled balloon at my brothers in revenge for their merciless bouts of picking on me. Then, suddenly, the door opened, revealing my father. I froze in fear, the water balloon attached to my privates. My dad stared in silence for a moment, then said, "First of all, you can't fill up a water balloon like that, dumbshit. Secondly, life is fucking long, especially if you're stupid." That phrase became a regular for him, one I've heard many times throughout my life. Holding that engagement ring in my hand made me think about just how long my life had already felt, and how many stupid things I had done. For the first time, it occurred to me that maybe I didn't know what I was doing.

Which is why, all these years later, I was looking to him for advice.

"You really like Amanda," I said to my dad, unsure if I was making a statement or asking a question.

"I mean, we haven't sat in a foxhole shooting at fucking Germans, but from what I know of her, yes, I like her a whole lot. But who gives a shit if I like her?" he said.

"I do."

"Bullshit. You don't give a rat's ass, and you know why?" he said, cocking his head and raising an eyebrow.

"Why?"

"Because no one in the history of relationships has ever given a flying fuck about what *other* people think about their relationships—until they're over," he said. "Now that's a pizza! Thank you kindly, ma'am," he chirped as the waitress dropped off our orders.

"Well, it's a big decision," I said, "so I'm trying to get some perspective. I just want to make sure I'm not making a mistake—that I'm not going to end up screwing her over, or me, you know? I think that's a pretty normal feeling most people have," I explained, suddenly feeling defensive and embarrassed.

"Most people are stupid. Nothing seems like a mistake until it's a mistake. You stand in front of an electric fence and whip your dick out to take a piss on it, it's pretty clear you're about to make a mistake. Other than that, you pretty much have no way of knowing."

I leaned back in the booth, quietly gratified that my dad still reached back twenty-five years, to the time when my brother urinated on our neighbor's electric fence, as his template for a mistake.

Between voracious bites of pizza, my dad noticed that I wasn't satisfied by his response, so he wiped his mouth and said, "All right. I'm gonna tell you two things. But neither of them is advice, okay? Advice is bullshit. It's just one asshole's opinion."

"Fair enough," I replied.

"First and foremost, I'm a scientist," he said, clearing his throat.

"I agree."

"I don't give a shit if you agree. It's not up for debate. I'm *telling* you: First and foremost, I'm a scientist. And as a scientist, I can't help but think about things critically. Sometimes it can be a curse. What I wouldn't give every once in a while to be a blithering idiot skipping through life with shit in my pants like it's a goddamned party."

I sprinkled red chili flakes on my barbecue chicken pizza and sat back to listen.

"So, scientifically speaking, marriage breaks down like this: There are six billion people on the planet. Say half are women. Now, taking into account age ranges and all that, even if you were picky—"

"I'm picky," I interrupted.

"I'm speaking universally, not about you specifically. The world doesn't constantly revolve around you. Just eat your fucking pizza and listen."

He waited silently until I grabbed a slice of pizza and shoved it in my mouth.

"Okay, so even if you were picky, you could probably be happily married to any one of a hundred and fifty million different women," he said.

This was surprising. My parents had been married thirty-two years, and my dad worshipped my mother. He was never shy about telling us that she came first. Once, when I was six, my dad put down a science journal he was reading over breakfast. It had a giant asteroid on the cover. He looked at me and my brothers and said, "If an asteroid hit the earth and it was a nuclear holocaust and the air was breathable, which it wouldn't be, I could be okay with your mother and I being the last two people alive."

"What about us?" my brother Evan asked.

"Well, I wouldn't just move on. There'd be a grieving period, obviously. I'm not an asshole," my dad replied before letting out a big belly laugh.

My dad loves my mother as if he has a biological need to be with her. So hearing him tell me casually that any one of us could be happily married to one hundred and fifty million different people seemed inconsistent with his own example.

"You don't buy that. I know you don't think you could have what you have with Mom with someone else," I said.

"I said I had two things to tell you. Now, *scientifically*, that's how it breaks down. But we're complex animals, and we're constantly changing. Things I thought ten years ago seem like absolute bullshit now. So there's no scientific formula to predict how things are going to work out with a marriage, because a marriage in year one is completely different from the same marriage ten years later. So when you're dealing with something incredibly unpredictable, like human beings, numbers and formulas don't mean shit. The best you can do is take all the information you have and, scientifically speaking, do what?" he asked, staring at me, awaiting an answer.

"Uh . . . I don't know," I said, unsure if this was a rhetorical question.

"I should buy you a fucking sign that says 'I don't know' to save you time. The best you can do is make an educated guess, son.

"So I'll tell you what I did right before I asked your mother to marry me: I took a day and I sat and I thought about all the things I had learned about myself, and about women, up to that point in my life. Just sat and thought. I may have smoked marijuana as well. Anyway, at the end of the day, I took stock of everything I'd gone through in my head, and I asked myself if I still wanted to propose to your mother. And I did. So that's what I humbly suggest you do, unless you think you're somehow smarter than I am, which, considering you share my genetics, is unlikely," he said, laughing as he sat back and took a big sip of Diet Coke.

I paid the tab and I dropped off my dad back at home.

The next day was the day I'd planned to propose to Amanda.

I had booked a flight to San Francisco, and arranged for her best friend to bring her to a restaurant for brunch, where I'd be waiting to surprise her and pop the question. From the time I dropped my dad off, I had exactly twenty-four hours until I was due to meet Amanda.

I got in my Honda Accord and drove to Balboa Park in downtown San Diego. When I got to the parking lot, I got out of my car and started walking in no particular direction. There, in the shadows of the large Spanish buildings that housed most of San Diego's museums, I spent the entire day doing just as my dad suggested: thinking as far back as I could remember and replaying every moment that had ever taught me anything about women and myself, from the awkwardness of childhood to the tribulations of adolescence and early manhood, in hopes that, before the day was done, I would know that the decision I was about to make was, at the very least, an educated guess.

I Like It

In elementary school, the first day of school is a big one for many reasons—mostly because it's when students find out where they'll be sitting for seven hours a day for the next nine months. One poor choice can doom a youngster's social life for the year. Three weeks before I entered second grade, my teacher, Mrs. Vanguard, a slender woman in her fifties with a haircut that made her look like George Washington, sent her students' parents a letter announcing that seats would be determined on a first-come, first-served basis. If ever there would be a Black-Friday-at-Walmart stampede of marauding seven-year-olds, this was surely it.

"I want to be there at six in the morning," I announced to my parents in our kitchen the evening before school started.

"Six A.M.? You running a fuckin' dairy farm? No. Not happening," my dad said.

I remembered what my friend Jeremy had told me that afternoon—that he was planning to be first in line outside the school doors at sunrise, to make sure he got the best possible seat—and started to work myself into a panic.

My mom looked at me sympathetically. "We'll get you there as early as we can, but not if you don't put some pants on before you come to dinner." My evening wear that night was a pair of Transformers tighty-whiteys and a T-shirt featuring Walter Mondale's silk-screened face over the slogan MONDALE'S GOT THE BEEF.

The next morning, when my dad woke me up the way he did every weekday morning—by ripping the covers off me and hurling them to the floor while loudly humming "The Ride of the Valkryies"—I burst out of my bed and looked at the clock. 7:30 A.M.! School started at 8:00!

"Dad, you said you'd wake me up really early!" I yelled in outrage.

"Bullshit. I distinctly remember saying I would do the exact opposite of that."

I got ready as fast as I could, but by the time my mom dropped me off at school and I sprinted to my classroom, clutching my backpack to my chest to maximize my speed, I was horrified to discover that there were only three empty seats left. I stood behind the thirty or so desks that faced the long green chalkboard at the front of the class and carefully considered my next move. The first empty seat was in the front row, directly facing Mrs. Vanguard's desk. That would be social suicide. No one wanted to come near her desk. It'd be like buying a house underneath a freeway overpass in Detroit. The second was next to a chubby kid who'd had two accidents in his pants the year before, both of which required the chair he was sitting in to be hosed off and disposed of in the Dumpster by a janitor wearing surgical gloves and a mask.

The third seat was next to a red-haired girl I'd never seen before. She had a smattering of freckles across her face and a button nose that made her look like she'd been created by a Disney animator. I didn't like girls—not because I thought they were gross or had cooties, but for the same reason I didn't like underwear: they seemed unnecessary and mildly annoying. But this seat appeared to be the least of the three evils, so I headed in that direction and slung my backpack over the chair. My red-haired classmate turned and smiled at me, and for some reason, I was taken aback. I tried to greet her, but my brain couldn't decide whether to say "hi" or "hello."

"Halo," I spluttered.

"Hi. I'm Kerry Thomason," she replied brightly.

That was all she said to me that day, but it was enough to make my stomach feel a little queasy. I didn't know why, but I wanted Kerry to pay attention to me. And, as the weeks went on, it seemed like antagonizing her was the best and most fun way to get her to do so. I spent that first week poking her sides with my pencil eraser, stealing her My Little Pony–themed Trapper Keeper, and generally doing anything I could to get her to notice me, except for actually speaking to her. The only words she said to me that week were "please stop," and that only made me want to keep doing whatever I was doing.

About two weeks into the school year, I finally pushed my luck too far. I brought into school a drawing I had spent half the night and a full carton of crayons creating and plopped it down on Kerry's desk before the first bell rang. She took one look at it and burst into tears. At the first sound of crying, Mrs. Vanguard popped her head up from her prepackaged weight-loss meal and rushed over to Kerry. She was asking Kerry what was wrong when she saw the drawing—and gasped in horror.

She turned to me and asked, "Did you do this?"

"Yes?" I responded hesitantly as I began to realize that my plot to impress Kerry might not come off as planned.

"That is disgusting," Mrs. Vanguard said. She grabbed my arm above the elbow, her fingers cutting off my circulation, and walked me straight down the hall to the principal's office.

I had never seen the inside of the principal's office before, but I'd always imagined it would be like a king's chamber in a palace, complete with fresh bowls of fruit, a throne, and a small disfigured man who did all the principal's bidding. Instead, the waiting room was disappointing: a drab ten-by-ten room featuring a framed poster of a bodybuilder struggling to deadlift a huge weight bar, captioned with the slogan BELIEVE IN YOURSELF AND ANYTHING IS POSSIBLE. Mrs. Vanguard dumped me in a metal folding chair next to a desk, behind which sat the principal's secretary, a short, squat woman in her sixties with a huge nose and ears like a fifty-year-old prizefighter. She looked at me and shook her head, and it was at that moment that I realized I was in pretty big trouble. I managed to keep my composure until Mrs. Vanguard said, "We're going to call your parents, Justin."

"No! Please, no," I said, starting to cry and shaking my head in fear like someone pleading with a killer for his life. She stepped out of the office, and when the door shut behind her it was so quiet that I could hear my heart pounding in unison with the ticking of the wall clock. The secretary consulted her ledger, picked up the phone, punched a few numbers, and said, "Can I speak to Mr. Halpern, please? It's about his son."

The hours that followed were some of the longest of my life. Every time I heard approaching footsteps, I was sure they belonged to my parents, and my muscles tensed in fear. As frightened as I was, though, I also found myself thinking about Kerry. I didn't want her to see I'd been crying, so I dried my tears with the backs of my hands and used my shirt cuffs to wipe the snot that was running down my nose. I thought about how she smiled at me on the first day of class. I thought about how I liked the way she dotted her I's with hearts, and the way she sneered at me every time she came back from the bathroom and I asked her if she had taken a poo. I thought about Kerry so intently during those two hours that I almost forgot how terrified I was that my parents were coming.

And then the door opened, and my dad entered. I had prayed my mom would arrive first, but she was never as punctual as my dad. He was carrying his brown leather briefcase, and his eyebrows were like two tiny arrows pointing almost straight down toward his nose. He was not happy.

"Okay, I'm here. What in hell is going on?" he asked, looking at me and then the principal's secretary.

I sat quietly, staring at the ground, avoiding eye contact with my father.

"Hi, Mr. Halpern. Thank you for coming," the secretary said.

"Yeah, no problem. Just a thirty-five-mile drive in the middle of my workday. Goddamn pleasure."

The secretary shot me a look, a silent cry for help. I glanced back at the floor; she was on her own.

"Uh . . . well . . . Justin acted incredibly inappropriately in class, and his teacher had no choice but to remove him," she said.

"Ah, hell. What'd he do? He pull out his pecker and show it to somebody?" my dad asked.

"Uh, no," the secretary said, between deep breaths. "His teacher will be with you shortly. She can explain," she added quickly.

My dad plopped himself down in a chair directly across from mine, so that he could focus his intense stare on me without any obstruction, and silently mouthed the words "You're in deep shit, chief." I don't think I saw him blink or look away once. A few minutes later, when my mom entered the small office, the secretary stood up from behind her desk, reopened the door, and walked us back down the hallway to my classroom. With every step my throat tightened. It was recess, so my classmates were playing outside; at least Kerry wouldn't be privy to my humiliation. When we got to the classroom Mrs. Vanguard was sitting behind her big wooden desk, and she motioned for us to sit down in front of her. As my mom and I quietly took our seats, my dad wrestled to squeeze himself into one of the tiny chairs. Finally he just said "Screw it" and sat on top of the desk.

"Mr. and Mrs. Halpern, this morning Justin gave this drawing he made to a girl he sits next to in class," my teacher said, sliding a piece of lined paper across the table to my mom and dad.

My parents both leaned in to examine it. My mom took one look and let out a sigh in disappointment. My dad leaned in for a closer look.

"Jesus, what the hell kind of drawing is this?" he said.

It was a crude drawing of a smiling, female stick figure with red hair and a T-shirt that read "Kerry." Above Kerry's head was a yellow dog. Those two elements alone, of course, would not have caused a problem. Unfortunately, there was a third element to the drawing: a shower of large brown clumps raining down from the yellow dog's rear onto Kerry's face. And just in case the viewer wasn't sure how Kerry felt about that, a thought bubble protruding from her head read, "I like it."

"It's very upsetting," my teacher said.

"Why is the dog above her head? That doesn't even make sense. How'd he get above her head?" he asked, turning to me.

"I don't know," I said.

"You have to draw a hill or something under the dog. A dog can't just float up into the atmosphere and take a shit on someone's head. I mean, I know you're six or seven or whatever, but that's pretty basic physics right there," he said.

"Mr. Halpern, that's really not the issue," my teacher said.

"I dunno, seems like a pretty big issue to me. At least we know we can cross *artist* off the list," he said.

"Sam, let her talk," my mom said, sternly. My dad leaned back, mumbled, "Not the issue, my ass," then sat silently. I listened as Mrs. Vanguard chronicled my behavior toward Kerry over the past two weeks, behavior she felt bordered on harassment. Without proper discipline, she told my parents, she feared I might turn dangerous. I wasn't sure what my feelings about Kerry meant, but as I listened to Mrs. Vanguard and recalled how I'd made Kerry cry, I suddenly felt terrible.

"Excuse me for saying this," my mom interrupted, "but I think you may have the wrong idea. It seems pretty clear what this is."

"And what would that be?" my teacher asked.

"He's sweet on her," my dad responded. "Jesus H. I woulda figured you see this kind of stuff all the time. Look, trust me, I know the kid can be dopey as all hell. I caught him eating a sandwich on the shitter just a month ago. But he's a sweet kid. He's not goddamn Manson."

My teacher sat there speechless until my mom broke the silence by assuring her that they would take me home at once and talk to me about my inappropriate behavior.

"We'll make sure this stops," she said.

I rode home with my mom, since my dad announced he'd just had his car cleaned and wished to keep it "booger-free for as long as fucking possible."

As she pulled into our driveway, my mom told me to go to my room and wait for her and my dad. About ten minutes later they both appeared. My mom sat next to me on my bed. My dad grabbed a chair, shook the Legos off it onto the ground, and sat down.

"Justy, do you know why you can't draw pictures like the one your teacher showed us?" she started.

"Yes. Dogs can't fly above people's heads," I said.

"No, honey, that's not why," my mom said.

"Well, that's part of the reason why," my dad said.

"No, Sam, you're confusing him."

"He's confusing me. He's got dogs flying around, people wearing fuckin' T-shirts with their names on them, like everybody works at a goddamn auto shop. All I'm saying is, there's multiple problems at work here. Let's not condone some fantasyland where—"

"Sam!"

My dad went silent and nodded.

"Do you like sitting next to Kerry?" my mom asked.

I nodded yes.

"All right. Well, from now on, if you like somebody, you don't do mean things to them, even if they seem like they don't like you back," she said.

"Okay."

"Lots of people will like you back in your life, Justy," my mom said, giving me a hug and then getting up to leave. "For today, though, you need to sit in your room and think about what we talked about."

My mom left the room, and a moment later my dad stood up to do the same. Just as he was about to close the door, though, I felt the need to apologize.

"I'm sorry I made Kerry cry," I said.

He turned around and looked me in the eye.

"I know you are. When you're sweet on a woman, you do crazy shit. It happens. You ain't used to feeling that way about somebody."

"I feel that way sometimes about Mom," I said.

"What? No you don't. Jesus, that's the creepiest goddamn thing you've ever said to me," he said, as he started to close the door.

"Wait," I said.

My dad stopped once again.

"Yeah?"

"What do I do now?" I said.

"What do you do with what?" he said.

"With Kerry."

"Jack shit. You're seven."

When You're Married, Your Wife Sees Your Penis

When I was little, my two favorite things were Cinnamon Toast Crunch cereal and learning new words. I was obsessed with expanding my vocabulary. Every time I heard a word I didn't recognize, I'd ask the nearest adult what it meant. No one had a more extensive vocabulary than my father, who spent a lot of time reading with me each night to indulge my thirst for language.

"My teacher says someday I'm going to know as many words as you do," I told him one night as we sat at the dinner table after I aced an oral test in my third-grade English class.

"Don't take this the wrong way, but your teacher is full of dog shit. I practice medicine, which opens up my vocabulary to thousands of words you will never encounter. I know a hundred goddamn ways to talk about blood vessels," he said, grabbing a bowl full of green beans and spooning a few onto his plate.

"That's really cool," I said.

"It's not cool. It makes my head want to explode. It's like a garage filled with useless shit. It ain't how many words you know, it's how you use them."

A couple days after that conversation, my dad was appointed head of his department, nuclear medicine, at the University of California, San Diego.

"So now you're the boss!" I said when he told my family the news over a spaghetti dinner.

I looked at my mom, expecting her to be excited, but she just looked tense and unhappy.

"Being the boss ain't always a good thing," my dad said as he took a sip of red wine.

"Why not?" I asked.

"You like playing baseball, right?"

"Yeah."

"Well, what if the coach quit one day and they made you coach because no one else wanted to do it? So you'd have to coach the team instead of being able to play, and then you'd have to sit and do all the bullshit that comes with coaching."

"Coach likes being the coach."

"That's because he's an asshole who's trying to live out his dreams through that kid of his, who's five years away from a fucking heroin addiction because his dad's a psycho."

"Sam, you know he's going to repeat that," my mom said.

"Don't repeat that," he said to me. "Anyway, my point is, I became a doctor to practice medicine and help people. Now I gotta sit in an office and do paperwork. Not your problem, it just means you're not going to see a lot of me."

After that, my dad started leaving for work before I woke and arriving back home after 9:00 P.M. He worked a full day most Saturdays, too. Sunday was his only day off, but even then he often went in to the office. Nevertheless, no matter how late it was when he walked through our front door or how tired he was, he would grab my favorite book, J. R. R. Tolkein's *The Hobbit,* and call me into the living room, flip on a lamp next to our brown fabric couch, sit down right next to me, where he'd read to me or I'd read to him. Whenever I encountered a word I didn't understand, I'd stop and ask him what it meant. One night, while I was reading to him, he started laughing.

"This might just be because I'm tired as hell, but you know what I just realized?" he asked.

"What?"

"Nobody ever gets laid in these Hobbit books. This thing spans Bilbo's whole goddamn life, but the guy never gets laid. Not once. No sex," he said.

"Bilbo doesn't have any kids," I said.

"What does that have to do with anything?" he asked.

"Well, if he had sex, then he'd have kids."

My dad let out a huge, long belly laugh.

"Jesus Christ. Thank God it doesn't work like that. I'd have populated fucking Rhode Island."

I didn't understand why my dad was laughing, and I was insulted by his mockery.

"You get married and then, if you want, you have sex and have kids," I said, firmly.

"If you want? Ha. Shit, don't tell your mother that or I'd never get laid. I don't think you know what marriage means," he said, laughing again.

"I know what it means. That's, like, a first-grade word. I've known what it means for a long time," I scoffed.

"I'm fairly certain you haven't the faintest goddamn clue, trust me," he replied.

"Fine. Then tell me what it means," I demanded.

"Son, I just worked fifteen hours, and I'm dog tired, and you don't have a single hair on your balls. I think that conversation can wait until one of those things changes."

The next day at school, as I sat in the cafeteria unpacking my lunch, I told my best friend, Aaron, what my dad had said about sex and marriage and asked him what he knew about the relationship between the two. A slender kid with shaggy brown hair and pasty white skin, Aaron grew up a few blocks from me. He had HBO, which instantly made him an expert about sex as far as I was concerned. He put down his Cheetos and wiped his hands on his University of Michigan Fab 5 basketball shirt.

"I can't believe you don't know this," Aaron said. "On the night you get married, you have to have sex, otherwise it doesn't count as getting married. It has nothing to do with babies," he added.

"I already knew that it didn't count unless you had sex. I already knew that," I lied.

"You're supposed to start kissing your wife, then she takes your penis and she puts it in her, and you have sex," he said.

"Does she see your penis?" I asked, panic creeping into my chest.

"No. They just put their hand down there and grab it, but they can't look at it and see it unless you tell them they can," Aaron answered.

I'm not sure if it was an adverse reaction to the fact that my dad often walked around our house in the nude like a *Playboy* playmate in Hefner's mansion, or if I was just self-conscious about my body, but there was nothing I hated more than the thought of someone seeing me naked. Not skinning my knees. Not pooping in public restrooms. Nothing.

My brothers were usually my go-to for information, and even though they almost always made up ridiculous answers to my questions in an effort to make me look stupid, I still went back to the well time after time. One Sunday morning, over breakfast, I asked them about the wedding night ritual. My brother Dan, who was well acquainted with my fear of nudity, was the first to weigh in.

"There's a little more to it than that," he said. "Basically, you stand in one corner of the room, and she stands in the other. You each take off one piece of clothing at a time. Pants and underwear go first," he said.

"Before shoes and socks?" I asked.

"Yep. You still have your wedding tuxedo on, you're just not wearing pants or underwear," he said, biting into a chocolate glazed donut.

This was troubling information. As soon as breakfast was over, I got up from the kitchen table and went into my bedroom and closed the door behind me. Then I put on the only suit I owned, and proceeded to remove my pants and underwear, keeping on my shoes and socks and everything from the waist up. Then I looked in the mirror. Of all the disturbing images I'd encountered to that point in my life, that image of my skinny, half-naked body landed somewhere between "when this weird kid Andre in my class turned his eyelids inside out" and "seeing a car run over the head of my neighbor's cat."

I couldn't stand the idea of someone else seeing me in this compromising position, laughing uncontrollably. But before I took a vow to be a bachelor for life, there was one thing left to do: ask the only person I knew who was married, always honest with me, and never mocked my fears—my mom. I changed out of my suit, threw on my Teenage Mutant Ninja Turtle pajamas, and ran to my parents' room and knocked on the door. There was no answer and the door was locked. I was fairly sure they were in there, but then again they could have left before I woke up. I went back into the kitchen where my brother Dan was now working on a big bowl of Cinnamon Toast Crunch.

"Do you know if Mom is here? Her door is locked and nobody said anything when I knocked," I said.

"Their bedroom door is locked?"

"Yeah."

"Just get a screwdriver and pop it open and see if they're in there. If they're sleeping they'll probably want to be woken up so they won't sleep in too late. You know how Dad hates that," he replied.

I should have sensed something was wrong, given my brother's surprisingly helpful response, but he had a point. My dad did hate sleeping in, and rarely if ever did it. Armed with that reminder, and still panicked at the prospect of my future wife seeing me in half a tuxedo, I ran to the garage and grabbed a screwdriver from my dad's toolbox.

The locks in our house were pop locks, easily opened by shoving a flathead screwdriver inside a tiny hole and turning. And so I did.

When I opened the door, I saw my mom and dad naked in bed together, one big entangled mess of middle-aged limbs and hair. Until that moment I didn't know what sex looked like, but I knew immediately that this was it. They both turned and looked at me and froze.

"I'm sorry!" I screamed.

I slammed the door, ran down the hall, and sought refuge in my bedroom. About five minutes later, my dad opened my door, wearing a black terrycloth robe, his face contorted in the expression you make between the moment when you stub your toe and the moment you say "ow."

"Your mom wants me to sit down and tell you what you just saw, but I'm currently not in the mood to give a shit, due to being thrown out of bed because my eight-year-old suddenly turned into Harry fucking Houdini."

We stared at each other blankly, each waiting for me to say something. I was still in shock.

"Well, I'm up, and my morning just took a left turn into a pile of shit, so you might as well tell me what has you picking my lock," he finally said.

I hurriedly explained to him my fears about wedding nights and sex and nakedness and the humiliation of having to wear socks and shoes but no pants or underwear.

"You do realize the irony in this situation, right?" he asked.

"What's irony mean?"

"You wanting to know about married people screwing and then walking in when . . . No. You're not back-dooring me into a conversation about this shit." He ran his fingers through his hair, and blew a deep breath out through his nose.

"All right. Here's the deal. You're eight," he said.

"I'm nine," I said.

"Do I look like I carry an abacus with your name on it? Cut me some slack here, son." He took another deep breath and started over. "What I'm trying to say is, you're just a little kid. I'm going to make you a promise. On your wedding night, you are not going to be able to wait until your wife sees your penis. Half a tuxedo on, no tuxedo on, socks, shoes, you won't fucking care."

"How can you be sure?" I asked.

"Trust me. You're going to be staring at your watch, wondering when this wedding is going to be over, so all these people will go on their merry fucking way so that your wife can see your penis."

"I will?" I asked, starting to feel comforted.

"Yep. And if you're still afraid that your wife is going to see your penis, that means she isn't the one for you. It also means you got a bunch of fucked-up issues and I totally screwed up, and then I'll pay for therapy if I have the money. But I probably won't. Anyway, for now, here's what the word marriage means: Don't pick the lock on my bedroom door on Sundays."

He got up, padded back down the hallway, and locked his bedroom door behind him.

You Will Never Screw a Woman Who Looks Like That

If you discount countless, forgettable chunks of time spent at school, home, and 7-Eleven, I passed most of my waking hours from ages ten through twelve playing baseball and goofing off with friends at the Point Loma Little League fields. Those two adjacent baseball fields were about a mile from my house, and twice a week my team, the San Diego Credit Union Padres, would gather there to practice.

"You should just be called the Padres, not all that bullshit about credit unions," my dad said, as he drove me to the field on the opening day of the season when I was eleven years old.

"But the credit union pays for us to have a team," I said.

"Yeah, well, I pay for you to do *everything*, and you don't see me making you wear a shirt with my giant goddamned face on it."

"That would be a weird shirt," I said.

"Please. You wear all kinds of dopey shirts, and—what the fuck am I talking about right here? The shirt's not real, I'm just making a point. You got your gear?" he asked, pulling up to the field.

Saturdays were filled with a full lineup of games, all of which the league's players were required to attend, so my parents could drop me off bright and early and then do whatever they wanted all day until my game. The prospect of a morning to himself was very exciting for my dad.

"There's a lot of good teams this year, I think," I said, continuing our conversation as we arrived at the fields.

He reached over me and popped open my door.

"Fascinating. Now out of the car. Vamoose. Out! Out! Have fun and don't screw with anyone bigger than you. I'll be in the stands when your game starts," he said.

I put my hand up for a high five, and he used that hand to push me out of the car. Then his Oldsmobile screeched away up the street, like he was fleeing the scene of a double homicide.

When we weren't playing in a game, most of the Little Leaguers would keep busy playing tag in between the two fields or eating a spicy linguiça sausage made by the local Portuguese family that ran the snack shack above the field.

Every once in a while, someone would raise talk of venturing into the canyon that sat about fifty yards beyond the outfield fences. We were all scared of the canyon. It was packed with trees that grew so close together their branches became intertwined like a bundle of snakes. The canyon's ground was muddy, and it emitted an odor that registered somewhere between "maple syrup" and "rest-stop bathroom." It was a group of cannibals short of being the perfect setting for an Indiana Jones film.

Every kid you ran into had a different theory about what lurked inside the canyon walls. "My brother found a pile of poo there that he said was too big to be dog poo or cat poo, but not big enough to be human poo. He said it's probably wolf poo," said my friend Steven as we waited for the game ahead of us to finish so we could take the field.

"Your brother's an idiot," said Michael, the chubby catcher on my team, who always wore his hat backward, so that the back of it came down right above his dark-green eyes. "A bunch of gays live in there. That's where they butt-fuck each other."

"What? Why wouldn't they do that at their house?" I asked.

"I don't know, I'm not a homo. But if you want to get butt-fucked, go into that canyon," he responded, inhaling a bite of sausage that would have killed a lesser twelve-year-old.

At that point in my life, the only two things that scared me were the movie *Arachnophobia* and that canyon. I tried to never get too close to it, for fear that something might reach out of the forest and pull me in. If I absolutely had to go near to chase an errant throw, my neck would stiffen and my breath would quicken as my body prepared to flee. I decided to run the theories about its inhabitants past my father to see if he had a scientific opinion on the matter.

"Why would gay people screw each other in a canyon filled with wolves?" my dad asked me as he drove us home after my game, my mom sitting beside him in the passenger seat.

"No, that's not what I said. One kid said there were wolves. It was a different kid who said the thing—"

"Hey, look at me, I'm screwing. My pants are off. Oh shit, there's an angry fucking wolf. Does that make any goddamn sense to you?"

"No. But that's not—"

"Plus," my dad interrupted again, "I don't even think wolves are indigenous to this area. Your school takes field trips. You ever heard them say shit to you about wolves? You gotta think about these things critically, son."

"No, I do. I didn't think that the wolves were—"

My mom turned to face me in the backseat. "Also, Justy, you know that homosexuals have sex just like heterosexuals do: in the privacy of their homes. Not in the woods."

"Although sometimes straight people do screw each other in the woods. Mostly when you're in high school, though," my dad added.

I decided to drop the conversation. But that week, on two consecutive nights, I had nightmares about the canyon. Each involved me finding something terrifying in a clearing at the center. In the first dream, I stumbled upon an aquarium that had a screaming Patrick Swayze trapped inside of it, begging me for help, but I was too scared to approach him. In the second, I was confronted by a large squid that had two or three sets of human legs. After that last dream I shot up out of bed, wide awake. I tried falling back to sleep, but every time I closed my eyes I pictured the canyon, then Swayze, then Squidman.

Hoping it would relax me, I tiptoed out of my bedroom to grab some water from the kitchen. I was still shaken from the dream, and the shapes of the shadows on the hallway wall looked ominous. Out of the corner of my eye I thought I saw something move, and I froze in place. *It's just a shadow that looks like a person*, I told myself. *It's not a person.*

"What in the hell are you doing?"

I shrieked like a frightened monkey and jumped back, crashing into the bookcase behind me. As my eyes adjusted I realized that the shadow was my dad, sitting in total darkness in the La-Z-Boy chair that faced the windows to our backyard.

"Jesus H. Christ. Calm down, son. What the hell is wrong with you?"

"I had a freaky dream," I said, trying to catch my breath. "What are *you* doing?"

"I'm sitting in the dark drinking a hot toddy. What the hell does it look like?"

"Why are you doing that right now? It's the middle of the night."

"Well, contrary to popular fucking belief, I enjoy a little time to myself, so I wake up early so I can have it. Clearly I'm going to have to start waking up earlier."

"Oh. Well, sorry. Didn't mean to bother you," I said, turning to head back to bed, glass of water forgotten.

"No apologies necessary," he said.

Maybe it was the bourbon in the hot toddy, or the serenity of the darkness all around him, but at that moment my dad seemed uncharacteristically at ease.

"Can I ask you a question?" I said, turning to face him again.

"Fire away."

"If something's freaking you out, what do you do to not freak out about it?"

"Is this about that *Arachnophobia* movie, again? I told you, a spider that large couldn't sustain itself in an urban environment. The ecosystem is too delicate. Not fucking plausible."

"It's not about *Arachnophobia*. It's just—if something's freaking you out, how do you get it to not freak you out?"

He raised his mug of hot toddy to his lips and took a big slurp.

"Well, scientifically speaking, human beings fear the unknown. So, whatever's freaking you out, grab it by the balls and say hello," he said.

I had no idea what that meant, and even in the dimly lit living room he could tell.

"I'm saying, if something's scaring you out, don't run from it. Find out everything you can about it. Then it ain't the unknown anymore and it ain't scary." He paused. "Or I guess it could be a shitload scarier. Mostly the former, though."

As I padded down the hallway back to my room, I knew what had to be done: I had to enter the canyon. There was just no way I was going it alone.

The next day I sat in my sixth-grade class watching the clock as the hour hand inched closer to 3:00. Michael was also in my class. He sat at the desk in front of mine, which meant that every day I spent eight hours face-to-face with whatever slogan was on the No Fear T-shirt he chose to wear that day. The inspirational messages printed on the backs of No Fear T-shirts all sounded like they'd been written by the president of a fraternity moments after he pounded his sixth beer. And the message on Michael's shirt that day was no exception: THERE'S NO SUCH THING AS UNNECESSARY ROUGHNESS. NO FEAR.

I tapped him on the shoulder. "Michael," I whispered.

Without looking behind him, he reached up with his left hand and grabbed my index and middle fingers, twisting them till I winced in pain.

"I just learned that in karate," he said, turning around, then letting go of my fingers. "I'm probably a year away from black belt."

I opened and closed my hand to get the feeling back in my fingertips.

"What's up?" he asked.

"You're going to baseball practice after school today, right?"

"Duh. I just got a new bat. It's part ceramic. It's awesome. You can touch it if you want," he said, pulling a bag from under his desk and unzipping it to show the blue-and-white bat inside.

He stared at me, then at the bat, then back at me, and I realized that his offer to let me touch it was more of a demand. We stared at each other for a moment, then I quickly poked it with my index finger.

He put the bat away. "Fucking awesome, right?" he asked.

"Yeah. It's cool. So anyway, I was thinking, since we both just go straight to practice after school, we could get there early today and go into the canyon."

Michael and I weren't friends, not exactly. He was a tough kid, the kind who spent most of his free time with older kids who had mustaches and were always throwing things at cars after school. But Michael was always willing to share with us what he'd learned from the older kids, and that was a real benefit to all of us.

I owed pretty much everything I knew about women at that point to Michael. During recess one day he pulled us into a corner of the yard behind the library and took out a folded-up picture. It was a page from a medical journal, featuring a photo of a forty-five-year-old naked woman, with possible postmenopausal cancerous areas highlighted on her body. Except for my mother, it was the first naked woman I'd ever seen. Michael pointed at the woman's crotch with his stubby finger. "That's where you stick your dick. They also pee out of that, and sometimes shit out of it if their butt's clogged."

It was this very wisdom and worldliness that inspired me to ask Michael to explore the canyon with me. I was, admittedly, a kid who was easily shaken. I wished I could be as fearless as my dad, but I seemed to have a different biological makeup when it came to courage. Michael was the only kid I knew who wasn't afraid of that canyon.

"So are you cool with going into the canyon with me?" I asked.

"I guess. If you buy me a Slurpee. Don't try and touch my dick, though."

One seventy-nine-cent stop at 7-Eleven later and we were walking toward the Little League field. The closer we got, the more I could feel the pit of nerves in my stomach tightening.

"So you've never gone really far into the canyon before?" I asked, trying to calm myself.

"Why are you so gay for the canyon?" Michael asked.

"I'm not. I just want to go in, look around, then come back out before practice."

"Are you retarded? You can't just go into the canyon and not know where the coach is," he said. "What if he gets to practice early, then sees us coming out of the canyon?"

"So what do we do?"

Michael quickly laid out a plan that seemed foolproof and tossed his thirty-two-ounce Slurpee container into a bush as we arrived at the empty field.

Sure enough, he was right about Coach. He'd arrived early for practice, and would surely have caught us sneaking out of the canyon if we'd opted for my plan. The rest of the team straggled in soon after. My friend Steven, who I always warmed up with, grabbed a ball and walked up to me.

"Ready to warm up?" he asked, popping a ball in and out of his glove.

"Not today. Go warm up with a big dick," Michael said to Steven, grabbing my arm and dragging me to the far end of the field. I glanced back at Steven and winked, assuming he'd understand that something was up and he shouldn't take it personally.

Michael and I started playing catch in the outfield. At any moment, Michael was going to say the code words and it would be go time. The anticipation was unbearable. I could barely hold on to the ball, my hands were trembling so badly with excitement. Suddenly, Michael's face hardened. He looked at the coach who was helping another kid about fifty feet away, then looked back at me and uttered the code words: "My dog peed in the house yesterday."

I took a deep breath, reached my arm back, and hurled the ball at least ten feet above Michael's head. It shot well past him and deep into the darkness of the canyon behind him.

"Coach!" Michael yelled.

Coach looked up from the lesson he was giving to another kid.

"Our ball went into the canyon. We're gonna go look for it, okay?"

"Fine. But if you can't find it quickly, come back up," Coach replied.

We nodded and jogged through the outfield and down the twenty-foot grass embankment that led to the canyon. At the bottom of the embankment we looked up. It was impossible for anyone on the field above to see us.

"Okay," said Michael.

"Okay," I replied.

"Okay what? This is your thing, shithead. What do you want to do?" he asked impatiently.

"Oh. Right."

I looked into the canyon, now just ten feet or so away. I could see past the first layer or two of tree branches and bushes, but beyond that it dropped off into darkness. I took a deep breath. *There is no Patrick Swayze in an aquarium,* I thought to myself. *There's no Squidman.*

"Okay. Let's go in through that part right there," I said, pointing to a small path that crawled through two trees.

Michael took the lead, and within twenty seconds we were deep enough into the canyon that when I turned to look back in the direction we had come from, all I could see were trees. The floor of the canyon was covered with dead leaves and some garbage: a few candy wrappers, a few empty 7-Eleven cups, which I strongly suspected had been hurled there by my comrade. My nerves were slowly subsiding. The farther we went, the less there was to look at. Just more trees, dead branches, and bushes. The unknown was quickly becoming known.

Michael was about ten feet to my right when he waved me over. "Whoa. Check this out," he said.

I hopped over a fallen tree and made my way over to him.

Michael moved aside, pulled back a couple branches, and pointed to what lay behind them. As he stood there holding it open for me, my mind started racing. *I do not want to look inside that hole*, I thought. *Yes, I do. I should look inside the hole. There's nothing there.*

"Hey. I'm not your branch-pulling guy, asshole. You gonna check this out or not?" Michael sniped, still holding back the brush as he waited for me to make a move.

I leaned forward and stuck my face into the opening Michael had created for me. Just past those branches lay a clearing, much like the ones I had seen in my dreams. Except this time there was no Patrick Swayze. In his place was a dirty sleeping bag and several blankets surrounded by garbage.

"I think somebody lives here," Michael said.

I could hear myself breathing in and out as my hands began to tremble once again, this time in fear.

"We should go back to practice. Coach is probably wondering—"

"Coach can suck a dick," Michael snapped.

He nudged me out of the way, pulled the branches farther open, stepped on the trunk of a fallen tree below him, and in one motion hopped through the small hole he'd created for himself. The branches snapped closed as I stood on the other side of the clearing. I could hear Michael walking around but couldn't see him. I stood motionless, hating myself for being frightened. Then the small window of branches reopened and Michael popped his head back through. "Are you seriously going to be a bitch?"

He grabbed my shirt and yanked me into the clearing. As I stumbled onto the other side of the branches, I realized that more than one person might be living here. There were piles of clothes caked with dirt, and empty cans of beer were strewn everywhere. Michael approached the sleeping bag surrounded by the trash pile.

"I think this is a bum cave," he said, nudging a couple of empty cans with his foot. Then something in the pile of trash next to the sleeping bag caught his attention. He knelt down beside it. Suddenly his head whipped.

"HOLY FUCKING SHIT."

"What?"

"It's the mother lode! Look at all this porno!" he shouted, shoving his hands into the pile like a pirate who'd found a trunk full of gold doubloons. With a look of pure ecstasy, he held up two handfuls of the dirtiest porn I could have imagined. There must have been a hundred more pages at his feet. I picked a few up and fanned them out in my hand. I had never seen so many pictures of beautiful women, let alone naked ones. I pumped my fist in the air like I'd just hit the game winning shot in the NBA Finals. This was my greatest accomplishment. The adolescent equivalent of landing on the moon.

At the time, porn magazines were like Lamborghinis: You knew they existed, and though you'd never seen one in person, you were sure you'd have one when you got older.

"I can't believe this. I just—man, we did it. We did it!" he screamed.

There was only one problem: What were we going to do with it all? Leaving it behind was not an option. After a few minutes of brainstorming, the best option we came up with was shoving the pages into our pants and keeping them there till we were through with practice.

Michael shoved a trial page in his pants, then took a step forward and backward, as if he was trying out a new pair of sneakers.

"It's too itchy," he declared. "New plan."

Eventually we decided the only option was to carry as much of the porn as we could out of the canyon and hide it beneath some leaves at the bottom of the embankment next to the field. After practice we could come back and get it. We started sorting through the loot, trying to decide which pages were must-takes.

Suddenly I heard a crack of a branch, as if caused by the weight of a foot. I jumped back, ready to run. We both looked around, but saw nothing. The silence was eerie.

"What if we just came back and got it later, or tomorrow, or next practice or something?" I said, fear creeping into my voice.

"Man, I like you pretty okay, but you're sort of a pussy. Just go wait outside the canyon and yell the code words if you see Coach. You remember the words, right?"

"My dog peed in the house yesterday," I muttered.

"Yeah."

As I walked out of the clearing, I was overwhelmed with shame. I had gone into the canyon to defeat my fears, but here I was, leaving the canyon because I was too afraid to stay. I stood there thinking, eyes downcast, till I heard Coach's voice.

"Justin. What are you doing?"

I looked up and saw him standing at the top of the embankment.

"I told you guys: Don't spend all day down there."

I froze for a split second, but then recovered.

"MY DOG PEED IN THE HOUSE!" I yelled.

"What?" Coach said.

Then, from behind me, I heard the rustle of bushes and the sound of heavy breathing. *Oh no, it's Michael*, I thought.

"MY DOG PEED IN THE HOUSE!" I yelled in that direction, terrified that Michael was about to walk out carrying a huge stack of pornography.

"What are you talking—"

Coach never got the chance to finish his sentence. In a flash, Michael burst through the bushes, running full speed ahead and clutching the porn to his chest like a woman holding her infant as she fled an explosion.

"RUNNNNNNN!!!!" he screamed in terror.

He ran right past me, and without giving it another thought I sprang into a full sprint, hot on his heels.

"What in the heck is going on?!" Coach yelled as we rushed up the embankment toward him.

I turned to look behind me.

There, hightailing it out of the canyon, came two bearded homeless men, each of whom looked like Nick Nolte rendered in beef jerky. I had never seen homeless guys move so fast and with such a sense of purpose. The last thing I saw on Coach's face as we blew past him was the look of a man who had no idea how the next fifteen seconds of his life were going to transpire.

The other players on the field turned to watch, mouths agape, as Michael and I sprinted by them, followed by Coach and the two homeless guys. Michael slowed down just a touch so that I could catch up.

"Take some!" he shouted, shoving a handful of pages at my chest.

"Go right! I'll go left. They can't catch both of us," he said between breaths, gearing back up to a full sprint.

I could hear a chorus of shouts behind us. I'm guessing it was one of the homeless guys and not Coach who hollered "Gimmie back my titties!" but I was too scared to look back and confirm. When I reached third base, I took a hard right turn and ran off the field and across the street. I didn't look back until one mile later, when I rounded the corner of my street and headed down the hill to my house. My legs were on fire and sweat poured down my face.

There were no cars in the driveway, so I made my way to the side of the house, unlocked the gate to our backyard, entered, then slammed it behind me, and for the first time in about ten minutes I stopped moving. I took the stack of porn, some of it now stuck to my chest with sweat, and placed it on the ground. I leaned over, put my hands on my knees, and gasped for air. I looked down at the bounty that lay at my feet, but my joy was soon displaced by fear. *What the heck am I going to do with all this?* I thought.

Then it hit me: like thousands of thieves before me, I would bury my loot. I ducked into my house, grabbed some newspaper, grabbed a shovel from our shed, and started digging in the corner of our backyard. After I'd dug a hole about a foot deep, I gathered every scrap of porn and placed the pile gently in the ground, as if I were planting a seed whose fruits I needed to feed my family. I placed newspaper over the pages and then filled in the hole.

Hours later I sat in front of the TV, wondering what had happened at practice, whether Coach had called my dad, and, most of all, what awaited me in those buried pages. I had gotten a quick look, but I wanted to pore over those pictures like they were evidence in a crime I was investigating. Eventually my dad got home from work and set his briefcase down.

"So. How was practice?" he asked.

"It was good. Why? Did you hear it wasn't?" I said, trying to keep my cool.

"Son, no offense, but you play Little League. It's not the Yankees. I don't get daily reports about who's hitting the shit out of the ball."

When I went to bed that night, all I could think about was those buried pages. I had worked hard for them, and I was determined to enjoy the fruits of my labor. I woke up in the middle of the night, and before I even opened my eyes, I thought, *The porno!* I hopped out of my bed, still in my underwear, and snuck out into the living room, through the back door, and into the backyard. I went to the shed, grabbed the shovel, found the spot with the freshly turned earth, jammed the nose of the shovel's blade into the ground, and started digging in the moonlight. My shoulders burned, but I kept digging.

"Son. What in the fuck are you doing?"

I shrieked, dropped the shovel, and turned to see my dad standing behind me in his robe, holding a hot toddy.

"Oh my God, you scared me," I said, completely forgetting that I should offer up some kind of excuse for what I was doing.

He clicked on the flashlight he was holding and shined it in my eyes, then down over the rest of my body.

"Please explain to me right now why you're in your underwear digging a fucking hole in my backyard at three-thirty in the goddamn morning."

There was no way out of this. I exhaled in defeat, then told him everything: about going into the canyon, finding the porn, running away from the homeless guys, then burying my loot.

He waited for a moment, processing everything, then quietly said, "All right, here's the deal."

Calmly but firmly, he instructed me to take all that porn out of his backyard and fill in the hole pronto. The next day, he explained, I would carry the magazine pages back to the entrance of the canyon and leave them there.

"Why can't I just throw them out? I don't want to go back to the canyon," I said.

"Bullshit. Someone spent time collecting this shit. What if I threw out your baseball card collection? That wouldn't be right."

I nodded. His analogy made sense to me, and suddenly I felt a twinge of remorse, having deprived those men of one of their few—and probably most prized—worldly possessions. I bent down and lifted the big wad of dirt-covered porno out of the hole.

"Are you mad?" I asked, as I picked up the shovel.

"Nah. I don't think this even cracks your greatest hits of stupid. But there's one important thing I need you to know."

I stopped shoveling and looked at him. He pointed at the pile of loose, grimy magazine pages on the ground.

"You will never screw a woman who looks like that. Understand?"

I nodded.

"Okay, good," he said. He turned back and walked toward the house, then quickly turned back around.

"And women aren't going to screw you in all those crazy ways, either. You got it? They don't look like that and they don't screw crazy. That's what you're taking away from this, okay?"

"Okay."

"Come inside and fill in that hole tomorrow. I don't want the neighbors thinking you're batshit."

I put down the shovel and followed him inside.

He sat down in his chair and turned on the small lamp next to him.

"The canyon was what I was freaked out about. That's why I went down there, so I wouldn't be freaked out about it," I confessed after a moment of silence.

"Son, you're a little on the jittery side. It's okay. Don't beat yourself up about it. It don't mean you don't have a pair of balls, it just means you're more choosy when you use them. That's not always a bad thing."

He took a big sip from his hot toddy.

"Are you going to bed now?" I asked.

"No, but you are," he said, turning off the lamp and filling the room with darkness. "I'm trying to get a damned minute to myself here."

Sometimes You Have to Be Hurled off a Diving Board Against Your Will

I spent the first couple years of high school trying to go unnoticed. My goal was to be the adolescent equivalent of one of those *Saturday Night Live* cast members who never seems to be in any sketches but is always on stage at the end of the show smiling and basking in the applause. I didn't start out so unambitious. Like most teenagers, I went in aspiring to be popular. But I realized that wouldn't be easy at a party early in freshman year. When my best friend Aaron and I walked into the party, the first guy we ran into took one look at us, removed the Bud Light from his lips, and shouted over the sound of Tupac blaring out of a nearby boom box: "What are you fags doing here?" His face showed the same genuine confusion you'd feel upon seeing a monkey operating a forklift at Costco.

Among my 2,500 classmates at Point Loma High School, I soon learned, there were popular people, unpopular people, and everybody else. Even just a couple weeks into high school, "everybody else" started to sound really good. Sure, maybe the popular kids were going to parties and getting hand jobs, but at least I wasn't being tormented. The key to becoming "everybody else" was to draw as little attention to myself as possible. I ate lunch with a small group of friends every day in the lobby of the English building, while the cool kids ate in the quad and the nerds ate in the drama building. I was a good student, but not so good that people noticed, and I spoke in class so rarely that during my sophomore year my history teacher pulled me aside and asked me if I was fluent in English in that loud, deliberate way people speak to foreigners. Although I excelled as a pitcher on the baseball team, few of my classmates cared about high school baseball or attended the games. And when the weekend rolled around, instead of going to parties, I would get together with Aaron and a couple of our friends, order in pizza, and watch '80s movies. By the start of my junior year, I had yet to go on a date, or even kiss a girl. But the older, popular kids had left me alone, and that was a tradeoff I was willing to accept.

The one person who wasn't so satisfied with my pathetic social life was my father. "You two are staring at that TV like you want to screw it," he said to me and Aaron one Friday night when he came across us watching *Die Hard* in his living room.

"Well . . . we don't," I replied, weakly.

"Thanks for clarifying that, chief," he said. He walked to the mahogany liquor cabinet next to the TV and poured himself a couple fingers' worth of bourbon. "I don't personally give two shits, but all I'm saying is, going out and drinking a beer and feeling a tit ain't the worst goddamn thing in the world." Then he padded back to his bedroom.

I shoveled another slice of pizza into my mouth and refocused on Bruce Willis, who was pulling broken glass out of his feet.

"Your dad's right. We need to go to parties," Aaron said.

"We're not invited to them," I replied, grabbing the remote control and turning the volume up.

We'd had this argument many times before. Aaron and I were now in our junior year and neither of us had been to a party since that very first embarrassment in ninth grade. Every so often Aaron would push me to go to a party or a dance, but it was as if there was a little sign in my brain reading, "It's been this many days since the last time you were humiliated," and I was determined to keep that number moving in the right direction. I had seen what had happened to some of my nerdier classmates when they dared to venture into social situations where they weren't welcome. One had been pinned down while someone drew penises all over his face in permanent marker. Another had been pantsed in front of the entire P.E. class. And since nothing like that had ever happened to me, I had talked myself into thinking that I was perfectly happy with the way things were.

In fact, I had done such a good job of it that when I turned sixteen, making me eligible for a driver's license, my parents had to force me to make an appointment to take the test. Unlike most teenagers, who long for the day they can get behind the wheel and drive with their friends to parties—or park somewhere and make out with their dates—I was indifferent about the prospect of getting my license. I lived less than a mile from school, and even closer to my friends' houses. With everywhere I went already within walking distance, a driver's license seemed like an unnecessary goal that could only be reached through an unbearably taxing process.

Nevertheless, at my parents' insistence, I looked up driving schools in the Yellow Pages and signed up for a course near my house that consisted of one two-hour lesson a week, for six weeks. My instructor was a skinny guy in his midtwenties who had a shaved head that was always peeling from sunburns and who could only have smelled more like marijuana if he'd been made of it. The training vehicle was a mid-'80s tan Nissan that had working brakes on the passenger side; he often got his jollies slamming them on for no reason and then between wheezing laughs saying, "You were all like 'I'm in control of the car' and then I hit the brakes and shit and you were all like 'Whaaaat?'" During one lesson, he had me drive him to "a buddy's house," then disappeared inside for half an hour; when he emerged he was so high he couldn't remember the way back to the driving school. We ended up driving around aimlessly for forty minutes while he told me about his life's goal, which was to prove that humans and sea lions could coexist on the beach. His plan centered on "eating a bunch of fish in front of them, so that, you know, they can see that we like fish, too."

Still, I managed to glean some driving knowledge from the course. So, one overcast Saturday morning in early October, I hopped into the passenger seat of my dad's silver 1986 Oldsmobile Brougham and we headed for the Clairemont Mesa DMV to take my driver's test.

"You excited?" my dad asked.

"Yeah, I guess."

"You guess? This is your independence right here. You get a license, you can take this car and never come back if you wanted."

"I could do that without a license," I said.

"No you couldn't, because it'd be illegal."

"Well, technically, so would taking your car and never coming back. That's grand theft auto," I said.

"Okay, let's just both shut up until we get to the DMV."

A few minutes later we pulled up to the tan one-story government building, which looked like the place where happiness went to die. Like most sensible Americans, my dad hates the DMV, and when we entered the lobby to find it packed to the gills with sweaty, tired, impatient people, he started nervously shifting his weight from foot to foot and biting his fingernails.

"Look at this fucking place. Everyone smells like dog shit, standing around like they're in Russia waiting for a loaf of fucking bread. Why the fuck am I here? You're the one taking the test." A minute later: "That's it. I can't do this. You're on your own," and just like that he took off for the exit. Before I could even respond he was sitting on a bench outside, reading the paper.

After a few minutes in line, I was handed a number by a morbidly obese receptionist. I sat down in the waiting area, which was filled with teenagers and the oldest people I had ever seen in my life. Thirty minutes later my number was called.

When I returned to the administration desk, I was greeted by a tan Korean man in his late forties wearing a white lab coat.

"Halpern, Justin?" he said, reading off a chart.

"I prefer to go by Justin Halpern," I joked.

He stared at me silently for a couple seconds. "This way," he said, then walked out a set of double doors and into the parking lot.

When we got into the car I tensed up. I hadn't been nervous before, but sitting in the driver's seat of my dad's Oldsmobile, without him in it, made me think for the first time about how exciting it would be if I were actually able to drive somewhere on my own. I could drive to movies, or school, or even on a date . . . and dates were where hand jobs happened. The array of opportunities flooded my mind, and I couldn't focus on the DMV examiner's nasal voice as he barked directions at me. I was gripping the steering wheel so tight my knuckles cramped, and every time he'd give me a direction, I repeated it back to him like we were doing an Abbott and Costello routine.

"Left here," he said.

"Left here?"

"Yes. Left here."

"Left here."

"Stop that," he snapped.

The low point of the test came when I tried to merge onto the freeway. In a panic, I drifted onto the shoulder, doing twenty-five miles an hour. "SPEED UP AND MERGE!" the examiner shouted. "OH MY GOD, SPEED UP AND MERGE." I had a feeling I'd failed—a feeling confirmed when I pulled back into the DMV parking lot and my administrator could only manage to spit, "YOU ARE . . . FAIL."

He got out of the car and slammed the door. I was mortified; any excitement I had about getting my driver's license evaporated immediately, and I decided once again that getting my license didn't really mean anything. After all, you don't need a license to eat pizza and watch old movies.

"It's not a big deal," I told my dad in the parking lot. "Honestly, I don't really even care. I'll just take it again sometime."

"Son, you're the only sixteen-year-old I've ever met who doesn't give a shit that he failed his driver's test. What do you think that says about you?"

"I'm levelheaded."

"That ain't what it says," he said, shaking his head.

In the days that followed, I didn't tell any of my friends that I'd failed my test; it was still too sore a subject.

That Friday, as I sat next to Aaron while we copied each other's answers before our first-period English class, a shadow fell on my desk. I looked up to see a classmate named Eduardo standing over me. I could count on one hand the number of times Eduardo had spoken to me in my life, but he'd made quite an impression. He was tall and thick, with slicked-back black hair that always looked like he'd just gotten out of a pool. He was also the only kid in our entire eleventh grade who had a real mustache. Those of us who were developed enough to even have facial hair grew thin, wispy mustaches generally associated with child molesters. But Eduardo's looked like a push broom, and it was terrifying. I only could assume he was there for one thing.

"Do you want to copy my homework?" I asked, handing him a piece of paper.

"What? Fuck nah. I do my homework on time. That's racist, fool," he said.

"Sorry, I was just trying to—"

"You know my cousin Jenny?" Eduardo interrupted.

"Jenny who?" I asked. There were lots of Jennys at our school, and I wanted to make sure I committed no further missteps in this conversation.

"Jenny Jiminez. She's in your public speaking class, fool."

"Jenny Jiminez is your cousin?" I was surprised. Jenny was sweet, and she had absolutely no facial hair.

"I'm Mexican. Everyone is my cousin."

"Ha! Look who's racist now . . ." I trailed off when Eduardo didn't even crack a smile. "Yeah, I know her. She's cool," I added.

"She likes your gumpy ass," he said.

And, with that, Eduardo retrieved from his pocket a small comb with a tiny wooden handle, ran it through his mustache exactly twice, then returned it to his pocket as he walked back to his seat.

"You should ask Jenny to homecoming," Aaron said, once Eduardo was a safe distance away.

"Yeah, right. I'm not going to homecoming," I said.

I hadn't gone to one dance in my entire high school career. I was six foot tall and a hundred and twenty pounds. When I danced, I looked like a praying mantis on fire. And besides, I already had plans for the Friday night of homecoming weekend: I was going to have Aaron over to watch *Predator* and *Predator 2*.

"Well, if you ask her, you guys can come with me and my date," Aaron said.

"What?" I said in disbelief. "You have a date for homecoming? When did you do that?"

"I asked Michelle Porter a couple days ago in math class. She said okay."

"I didn't even know you liked Michelle Porter."

"I've told you before that I thought she was nice and she has big titties," he said.

"Dude. There is a *huge* difference between saying someone is nice and that they have big titties, and asking them to a dance without telling me, okay?" I snapped back.

"What is your problem? Why aren't you happy for me?" he asked.

Aaron was right. I should have been happy for him and I knew it, but I felt angry and betrayed. His burgeoning social life was putting me to shame. Now, the thought of staying home and watching movies on the night of the homecoming dance made me feel like a total loser. I had to make a move.

"Fine. Then I'll ask Jenny to the dance," I said, in maybe the least confident way I have ever said anything.

"Well, if she says yes, then you guys can ride with us," Aaron replied.

"I don't want to ride in the back of your mom's minivan with my date, dude."

"Two seconds ago you didn't even want to go! I was just trying to be nice 'cause you don't have a license, asshole."

"I'll get my license. Also, I failed my first driver's test last week, and I'm telling you that now because I tell you things because we're friends and I don't just spring stuff on you," I spluttered.

* * *

As I walked home from school later that day, I realized I'd set myself two intimidating goals to accomplish in the next three weeks: asking a girl to a dance for the first time ever and passing my driver's test. I decided to start with the less daunting of the two: getting my license. Unbeknownst to me, my dad had already put a lot of thought into the problem.

Around 3:30 that day, I walked in the door to find him home from work early, and in his "action" sweatpants, which he usually only breaks out when he's trying to kill an animal in the backyard or perform some feat of strength around the house. They were grey, like most of his others, but they sported blue and yellow stripes down the sides and elastic around the ankles, presumably for aerodynamic purposes. As soon as I entered the living room, he stared me down.

"You, my friend, are going to learn how to drive because I am going to teach you how to drive," he said, the veins in his neck already starting to bulge.

My dad approaches teaching like it's a fight. He sees his students as opponents, and he pummels them with one piece of information after another until they're thoroughly disoriented and confused. Once the fight starts, no tapping out is allowed. He ordered me to drop my backpack and follow him to my brother's old GMC truck, parked in our driveway. He opened the passenger door for me like a very angry chauffeur, got behind the wheel himself, and nanoseconds later we were screeching up the street.

As he put the car into second gear, I made a troubling observation. "This is a stick shift," I said.

"Well done."

"But I don't know how to drive a stick. I learned on an automatic," I said, as he aggressively shifted gears.

"You remember when you were six or seven and we went to visit Aunt Naomi? We went to that pool with all the diving boards and you wanted to jump off of it, but you were too scared?"

"Yes."

"You remember what I did?"

"Yes. You carried me to the highest diving board in the entire place, grabbed me by the back of my swim trunks, and hurled me into the water."

"I tossed you off that thing like a sack of fuckin' potatoes," he chuckled as he stared out his window, reminiscing.

"What's your point?" I said.

"After that you went apeshit, jumping off every board in the place. You learn stick shift with me, you won't give two shits when you take the test in an automatic with some asshole in a lab coat. Make sense?"

"No."

"Too fucking bad," he said.

We drove to the parking lot of a nearby Circuit City, where he pulled the keys from the ignition and we switched seats. He gave me a quick overview of the gears and then spent the next hour screaming numbers at me, trying to train me to shift gears. "Three! Four! Six! There is no fucking six! Pay attention! Back to three!" I never even turned the car on.

Every day for the next two weeks, my dad went to work at six in the morning so he could leave early, come home, and give me a driving lesson before sunset. He began each lesson by announcing a theme for the day. Among them were "A car is a murder weapon," "Announce your presence with fucking authority," and my personal favorite: "Your mother is bleeding to death."

He said this late one afternoon as I pulled the truck out of the driveway. "If the shit goes down and you need to be across town in ten minutes without breaking the law, can . . . you . . . do it?" he added, lifting his eyebrows.

"I would just call 911 if that happened."

"Right. That's a fair point. But just bear with me, okay?"

"Okay, but that's not the kind of driving I'm going to have to do for the test."

"No. But I'm not teaching you to pass the test. I'm teaching you how to drive. Driving is not always a stroll through the woods with your pants down. Now, I want you to get from here to Clairemont in less than ten minutes. No illegal shit."

"Clairemont's ten miles away. I don't—"

"Clock starts in three, two, one!" he yelled, looking at his watch.

"Dad. This is not a helpful driving lesson."

"Nine fifty-nine, nine fifty-eight, nine fifty-seven, CLOCK IS RUNNING GO GO GO GO GO GO GO GO!" He kept screaming until finally I jammed the car into reverse, then back into first gear, and gave the gas pedal everything I had as we headed up the street.

I raced through the suburban streets of our neighborhood and toward the 5-North freeway that led to Clairemont. With the exactitude of the clown-faced, wheelchaired psychopath in the *Saw* movies, my dad explained the rules of the game: I wasn't allowed to exceed the speed limit, so in order to reach our destination in time, whenever I encountered a yellow light I should gun it, and whenever I approached a red I should decide quickly whether to wait it out or turn and take another route. Periodically my dad would scream how much time I had left, along with a new imaginary scenario that might be responsible for my rush.

"Six-thirty mark! Your buddy has kidney stones and he's in incredible pain!" he yelled as I hit the gas to make it through a yellow light.

I could feel sweat beginning to build on my forehead and my heart was racing.

"Three minutes! Your wife's car broke down in a bad neighborhood and she's afraid she's going to be sexually assaulted!"

"Stop! You're not helping," I yelled back as I weaved in and out of traffic toward the freeway exit for Clairemont. I gunned it past a semi in the exit lane and whizzed down the on-ramp. I just had to drive up hilly Balboa Avenue and I'd be in Clairemont. I figured I had about a minute left. There was one light halfway up the hill that stood between me and victory, and at the moment it was green, but I was still three hundred yards away. I kept waiting for it to turn yellow, but even a hundred yards away it remained green. Afraid it would turn yellow before I got close enough to race through, I started slowing down.

"What are you doing? It's green," my dad said, pointing at the light.

"I know, but I think it's going to turn yellow," I said, brushing sweat from my eyes.

"But it ain't. You're almost there. Come on now."

I hit the gas, but just as I did the light finally turned yellow. I panicked, convinced I was still too far away to get through it safely, but driving too fast to stop in time. Paralyzed by indecision, I froze, my foot leaden on the gas pedal. As the light turned red, our truck raced into the intersection and toward an oncoming Nissan hatchback. My dad reached over, grabbed the wheel, and pulled it hard toward him, causing the truck to jerk right and narrowly miss a collision.

"I can't believe you grabbed the wheel. I can't believe you grabbed the wheel," I said, mumbling like an insane person, once I'd hit the brakes and pulled over.

"You weren't doing anything. I had to do something," he said.

I wiped my face dry with my T-shirt. "I'm sorry. I'm really sorry," I said, feeling embarrassed at my incompetence.

"It's all right," he said.

By the end of the second week of my dad's driving school, I felt prepared to retake the state test, even if he wasn't convinced that I'd be able to get my future four-year-old son to the emergency room before he hemorrhaged to death. I had scheduled a second test, and felt like I had a real shot at getting my license this time, but my dad had been working me so hard I'd mostly forgotten that the end goal was being able to drive to homecoming. With the dance now only a week away, I realized I had to start working on the second part of my plan: landing a date.

Eduardo had said his cousin Jenny liked me, but then Eduardo had also told me once that he was taking woodshop so that he could "build a wooden knife and stab you, fool." I thought Jenny was cute, but I'd never asked a girl out before, and the thought of getting rejected—coupled with the threat of being stabbed with a shoddily made wooden knife for disrespecting Eduardo's cousin—was concerning. I decided to talk it over with Aaron at lunch the Monday before the dance.

"He never ended up making that knife. He made a bird feeder for his *abuela*," Aaron said as he wolfed down an avocado sandwich.

"Still, it doesn't make me trust him," I said.

"Just talk to Jenny. Wait for the right time, then ask."

"But I don't want to ask her if she doesn't like me. What do you think I should look for? Just eye contact and stuff like that?"

"Dude. I eat lunch with you every day and masturbate like ten times a week. I have no fucking clue. Just ask her."

Later that afternoon, I walked into my public speaking classroom, sat down behind Jenny, and waited for the right moment. I'm not sure how I thought the right moment would make itself known, but apparently it never did. In fact, I was so nervous at the prospect of asking her out that I couldn't even talk to her about class-related things. At one point, we had to break into small groups to formulate our arguments for and against legalizing drugs. When Jenny asked me to contribute, I said, "I like drugs, but also I don't like them," then immediately got up and walked out of class to the bathroom, where I paced around for a couple minutes to make it seem like I'd actually left the room for a purpose.

After three straight days of staring at the back of Jenny's head, trying to figure out what I should say, I finally worked up the nerve to attempt a conversation with her. I was confident that I'd come up with a pretty solid opener.

"Have you ever taken Flaming Hot Cheetos and dumped nacho cheese on them?"

"Yeah. It's good," she said.

"Yeah."

I said nothing else to her for the remaining fifty-four minutes of class.

On the walk home from school that day, I started to panic. There were two days left until the dance, and if I didn't get a date fast I was going to be sitting at home watching movies on my own when Friday rolled around. Aaron's move had spurred all of our other friends to take the plunge and get dates of their own and the thought of me watching *Predator* by myself made me ill.

I was so preoccupied with anxiety over homecoming that it wasn't until I walked into my house, and saw my dad holding his car keys with a big smile on his face, that I remembered that today was the day of my second driver's test.

"Let's shove this test up the DMV's ass," he shouted. He tossed me the keys to the Oldsmobile and led me out of the house. He grabbed the newspaper on our front lawn, opened the door to the backseat, and got in.

"Why aren't you sitting in the front seat?" I asked.

"I've always wanted to be chauffeured. Two birds, one stone," he said, reaching out and pulling the door shut.

I climbed into the driver's seat, started up the big silver sedan, and began my drive to the DMV. My dad opened up his newspaper and read in silence for a few moments before flipping down the top half of the paper and catching my eye in the rearview mirror.

"Hey, real quick. I don't want to flood your brain with a bunch of shit, but can I give you one piece of advice?" he said.

"Sure."

"Don't trust your instincts."

"What?"

"Your instincts are dog shit," he said, then went back to his newspaper.

"You're just gonna say something like that and then start reading the paper?!"

"Well, it's not really getting chauffeured if you don't get to do something like read the paper," he said.

"That is a messed-up thing to say to me right before the test!" I yelled.

He flipped the newspaper back down, revealing a quizzical expression.

"What crawled up your ass?"

"You did," I said, starting to get flustered.

"Look, calm down. It wasn't a dig. I just mean that every time you're uncomfortable and you get the option to sit something out, you sit it out. So all I was saying to you was: when your asshole gets tight, don't listen to your gut, 'cause you've filled it with shit."

He flipped the newspaper up once more and we rode the rest of the way to the DMV in silence. I was seething with anger the whole way there, thinking about what my dad had said. "I don't always sit things out. He doesn't even know what I do. He's only around me an hour a day," I told myself, getting angrier by the minute.

My father's voice reverberated in my head for the next hour, as I left him outside, checked in at the DMV, and sat in the waiting room alone. It followed me as my name was called, I led my lab coat–wearing test administrator to my car, and my test began. The truth is, I had no answer for my dad's accusation, and it infuriated me. With the DMV employee in the passenger seat next to me, I merged onto the freeway, but this time I was so preoccupied that I did so seamlessly. I was hell-bent on trying to find an example of when I had been confronted with something tough and not sat it out. Eventually, my thoughts led to asking Jenny to the homecoming dance. "That was something tough, and I didn't sit *that* out," I thought, as I turned onto the freeway exit and made a complete stop at the stop sign. Then I remembered that I hadn't actually *asked* Jenny out yet. I'd only *decided* to ask her out. Deflated, I made a left and pulled back into the DMV's parking lot. I felt like a total loser.

"You passed. Congratulations," the test administrator said as I put the car in park.

At first I didn't even hear him. Then he said it again and it sunk in. I had passed my driver's test. I had accomplished one of my two goals. My dad was wrong. I got out of the car and slammed my door in triumph.

"I passed my test," I announced to my dad as I met him outside in the DMV parking lot.

"Hot damn! Well done," he said.

"So take that!" I said, pointing at him.

"Take what?" he said, his eyebrows wrinkled in confusion.

"You didn't think I could do it. And I did it. Because guess what? I can do a lot of things that you don't think I can do," I said triumphantly.

"Uh, okay. I got no idea what in the fuck you're talking about, but whatever floats your boat, son."

I felt empowered, like one of those women in a Lifetime Channel movie who stands up to her husband. Now I just had to ask Jenny to the dance.

The next day, I strode into my public speaking class and sat in front of Jenny with a sense of purpose. There would be no more pussyfooting about; I was going to straight up ask her to the dance. I swiveled in my seat to face her.

"Hey, uh, Jenny, do you . . . like where you live?"

"Um, yeah," she said.

"Cool," I said, turning back around to face forward.

I took a deep breath and swiveled once more.

"So, uh, I don't know if you know the dance, or if not that's cool too?"

"Do I know the dance?"

"I was thinking . . . I didn't know if you had a date to the dance, or if someone asked you or not, but if they didn't or if they did and you said no, or whatever, I was wondering if you wanted . . . or if I could take you to the dance tomorrow."

That was the best she was going to get from me. I sat back and awaited her answer.

"Yeah, okay," she said.

"Awesome," I said.

I turned back around to find our teacher looking at me. I was so exhilarated I gave her a thumbs-up and spent the rest of the period replaying my victory in my head over and over, enjoying every minute of it.

"Dad, I have a date for homecoming, so I'm going to need the car," I said proudly when he got home that evening.

"Good for you! Congratulations, son. But tough shit. My car's not a fuck palace. I'll give you some money to take a taxi."

The next night, on the way home from the dance, in the back of a taxi cab driven by a guy who looked like Ernest Hemingway with a meth addiction, with Snow's "Informer" playing on the radio, I leaned in and kissed Jenny on the lips. It was my first kiss.

Could You Please Hand Me that Bottle of Peppermint Schnapps?

If there was anything that thousands of hours of movies had taught me, it was that prom was where awesome stuff happened. It was where virginities would be lost, scores with bullies would be settled, a hugely popular band could show up unannounced and perform, and a nerdy guy could get the prom queen. As the end of my senior year of high school approached, while some classmates focused on summer plans or leaving the state to go to college, I was hell-bent on having the most awesome prom imaginable.

The first and most important item on the checklist was finding the right date. I didn't usually shoot for the stars when scouting women;

normally I'd only ask a girl out if I found out she liked me. I'd hone in on the characteristic I liked—or, at least, didn't find objectionable—about her and use it to talk myself into how great our chemistry was. It was like deciding that the Olive Garden is the greatest restaurant in the world because it always has plenty of parking. But prom was the Super Bowl of high school, and I was determined to land a date who would help make it the night I'd been dreaming about for years.

My target was Nicole D'Amina, who sat a few seats away from me in my first-period A.P. English class. She was smart, mature, and composed, but not above my friends' brand of sophomoric humor. She had won me over on a Monday morning earlier in the year when she let out a blast of laughter after our English teacher said, "Sorry for the smell. Construction workers came in over the weekend and lined the walls with caulk." With dark brown hair down to her shoulders, sparkly green eyes, and olive skin, she was also incredibly hot.

"She has a ridiculous ass, man. It's crazy. It is a crazy ass," my friend Dan said to me as we walked out of class one morning during our senior spring.

"It is. She's super cool, too. I was thinking of asking her to prom."

"I'm not trying to be a dick, but she's not going to prom with you. She fucks college dudes."

"You know that for sure?" I asked.

"Not really. I just made that up. But she *seems* like she fucks college dudes. Like, I could picture a college dude fucking her, but I can't picture you fucking her."

I couldn't picture me having sex with her either. Then again, I couldn't really picture me having sex with anyone. I had never even

touched a bare boob. Since my first kiss, I'd gone on a few dates, had
a couple make-out sessions, and done enough dry humping to cause
a rash on my thigh. But I was ready to move forward.

"I'm just gonna ask her. If she says no, she says no. No big deal,"
I persisted.

"Yeah, but if she says no, then all the girls will find out, 'cause
that's the kind of stuff they talk about. Then, when you try and ask
another one of them, they'll know they're sloppy seconds and say no."

I resented Dan's pronouncement that he had "dropped a fuckin'
logic bomb" on me, but he had a point. I didn't want to risk missing
what could be the greatest night of my life by overshooting and asking
someone out of my league. Within minutes, I'd scrapped my original
plan to ask Nicole, and decided to ask someone I knew would say yes.

That not-so-special someone was a classmate named Samantha,
who was small and thin, with dark sunken eyes that made her look
like a creature out of a Tim Burton movie. She and I were usually the
first people to arrive at our English class, and she often came over to
my desk and asked me how I was doing and whether I needed any
help with my homework. She rarely talked to anyone else, so I was
pretty sure she had a crush on me.

The next day, I waited until our first-period class was over and
caught up with her as she was walking out of the room.

"Hey, Samantha," I said, following her through the doorway.

"Hey. What's up?" she replied brightly as we strolled out into the
quad.

"I was wondering if you wanted to go to the prom with me," I said
confidently.

"Uh, I . . ."

As her voice trailed off, she started picking up speed.

I tried to keep pace. "Did you hear what I said?" I asked between breaths.

But then her walk turned into a jog, and then into a full sprint, zigzagging through the crowd like she was returning a punt in the NFL. Within ten seconds she was fifty feet ahead of me. I sprinted after her for a while, but she kept running, and ten seconds later she faked left, then made a hard right, and was gone.

A few hours later, in sixth-period P.E., I sat in the bleachers of the football field with Dan and our friend Robbie, lacing up our running shoes for a jog, and explained what had happened.

"What in the fuck?" Robbie said.

"Yeah, she just took off running," I said.

"Why did you chase after her like a rapist?" Dan asked.

"I just chased her. I didn't do it like a rapist," I snapped.

Privately, I was surprised and hurt that Samantha wasn't the shoo-in I'd taken her for. And with only nine days till prom, I was still dateless and starting to worry. Still stinging from the rejection the next day, I tried commiserating with a classmate who, I'd heard, was the only other guy in our class who didn't have a date, a tough, stocky Filipino guy named Angel. Before fifth period, I turned to him and said, "Girls are so picky with this prom crap, huh?"

"Maybe with your skinny ass. I got a date last week, homey. She's from my neighborhood. My brother says she likes to fuck without rubbers," he said proudly.

I was officially the last man standing.

"I'll go with you," said a quiet voice.

I turned around to see Robbie's ex-girlfriend, Vanessa, who sat behind me. Robbie had broken up with her a few months back because, as he said, "I think each of us thought the other one was dumb." Her offer seemed a little strange to me, and maybe she wasn't Nicole, but she was cute and Robbie had always said, "She gets crazy." In light of her offer, I entertained a brief fantasy in which "getting crazy" involved drinking, dancing, boob touching, and maybe even virginity taking. I smiled at Vanessa and said I'd need to talk with Robbie but would love to go to prom with her.

As we were walking to baseball practice after school, I asked Robbie if he was okay with me taking his ex.

"You can do her in the butt for all I care. I'm totally fine with it," he said.

And so I accepted Vanessa's gracious offer the next day in class.

"I just don't want to go in a limo with Robbie and your friends," she said, picking at the eraser on her pencil. "It has nothing to do with Robbie, though. You can tell him that," she added.

I was disappointed that I couldn't ride to prom with all my buddies and their dates, but I was going with a cute girl and optimistic that it still might be the best night of my life.

The following Friday evening, I drove the two miles to Vanessa's house and picked her up in my mom's 1992 Oldsmobile Achieva. I was wide-eyed with excitement. And also really sweaty, to the point that I pulled the car over right before I got to her house, unbuttoned my shirt, and toweled off my armpits with an old T-shirt. Vanessa looked fantastic. She was wearing smoky black eyeliner, and her hair looked like a thousand golden curly fries. I was wearing a black and white tuxedo I'd rented from the mall; it was two sizes too big, but I chose it because the teenage salesman told me I looked "like a straight-up pimp with a degree in pimping" when I tried it on. My dad thought I looked like "a penguin with AIDS."

Before we took off, Vanessa's mom asked to take a picture. "Put your arm around her," she barked from behind her camera while the two of us posed awkwardly in their driveway. My palms were sweating from excitement, and when I removed my arm from around Vanessa's shoulder, I saw a dark spot on her dress where my hand had been.

On the ride to the prom Vanessa was strangely silent. I fiddled with the A.C. for a while and then finally tried to break the ice.

"Everything okay?" I asked cheerfully.

"What did Robbie say when you told him you were going to prom with me?" she asked.

"He said he was fine with it," I responded tentatively.

"That's it? He said he was fine with it?"

"Yeah."

"What did he say *exactly*?" she asked again, the muscles in her jaws clenching.

I recalled the butt-sex comment and gulped. "That was the only thing he said. That he was fine with it," I repeated.

"All he said was 'I'm fine with it?' He must have said *something* else."

"That's it. That's all he said. I swear."

"FUCK HIM! He's fine with it? He's *not* fine with it! He's a fuck-ing lying piece of shit!"

We sat quietly in the car as she stared out the window looking like a convict being hauled off to prison. When we arrived at the glass-walled downtown San Diego hotel where our prom was being held, I parked my mom's car in the underground lot and reached under the seat to grab the bottle of peppermint Schnapps I'd bribed a homeless man to buy for me earlier that day. I offered Vanessa the first drink and she grabbed the handle and pounded it like she was trying to forget a memory from the Vietnam War. We traded swigs in complete silence for the next five minutes until I couldn't feel my face. Then I tucked the near-empty bottle back under my seat and we got out and started walking toward the elevator.

As the Schnapps started kicking in, I began feeling a little con-frontational.

"You didn't really want to go with me, huh?"

Vanessa turned to me with a look of disbelief.

"Are you a retard? My ex-boyfriend is in there with some other girl," she said, starting to cry. "I need to sit down or I'm gonna puke," she added.

We wobbled across the dirty red carpet through the hotel lobby, decorated with tacky brass lamps, green polyester chairs, and a few women I assumed were prostitutes. As we walked past them, one raised her hand to her nostril, covered it with her thumb, and blew a snot rocket onto the ground by her feet.

We pushed through two double doors at the far end of the lobby and entered a huge dark ballroom that contained three hundred or so of our classmates swaying to the chorus of "End of the Road" by Boyz II Men. Our class had voted for a Rastafarian prom theme, so the room was strewn with pictures of Bob Marley and stickers that said "One Love," most of which had been defaced so that "one" was crossed out and "Butt" was written in its place.

Vanessa and I sat on the opposite side of the room from the dance floor, near a spread of stale chips and crackers, curdled dips, and cheese cubes from Safeway. That was where we remained for the rest of the night, mostly in silence, watching our classmates laughing, dancing, and chatting it up while Puff Daddy's "I'll Be Missing You" and "Return of the Mack" played on continuous loop. The scowl on Vanessa's face made sure none of my friends came near us, which, I'm pretty sure, was her goal. Nicole passed us a few times on the way to the bathroom, and though I wanted to say something to her, all I could muster was a smile. The dream of a dancing, boob-touching, bully-punching, virginity-losing prom was now dead, and there was no other way to spin it. I was disappointed and felt stupid for letting myself get so excited about one dumb night and for thinking it might be any different than the rest of high school. I slumped down in my chair and shoved a handful of nacho cheese Doritos into my mouth.

By the time the DJ announced the next song would be the last, most people had been sweating through their tuxedos and dresses for hours, and the whole place smelled like a bathroom stall in a public library. As Dave Matthews's "Crash" began to play, all my classmates grabbed their partners and made their way to the dance floor—but one look from Vanessa told me I should follow her to the nearest exit and take her home.

"I'm drunk," she hiccuped after a few minutes of driving in silence. "I'm sorry I called you a retard. I hope I didn't ruin your night," she added. When we arrived at her house, she got out of my mom's car and walked up her steps without looking back.

As I sat there in the car watching her front door close behind her, I took a deep breath. It was ten P.M. and my senior prom was the exact opposite of everything I'd hoped. Even in the worst-case scenarios I'd dreamt up, it had all gone wrong because I'd punched out somebody I hated and gotten dragged away by the cops. This was a total letdown.

I couldn't let the night end this way. I decided to turn my car around and head back toward the San Diego harbor, where the school-sanctioned, casino-themed after-party was being held at a restaurant called the Bali Hai.

When I got there, my sophomore history teacher, Mr. Bartess, was standing at the door with a clipboard. He glanced at me, scanned the clipboard, and shook his head.

"I have you marked as being here already. I'm sorry, no ins and outs. It says so on your ticket. We can't have people leaving to go do cocaine or something and then coming back in here, on cocaine," he said.

"But I haven't been here. And I don't do cocaine."

"Listen, you might be right, but that also sounds like something someone who left the after-prom to do cocaine would say. That's why we have no ins and outs, so I don't have to be the judge."

I didn't have the energy to keep arguing. The muffled sounds of music and laughter inside the Bali Hai drifted away as I walked along the boardwalk, which hovered just ten feet above the glassy ocean surface, back toward the lot where I'd parked. It was pitch-black out, save for the lights of the skyline glowing across the bay.

As I neared my parking spot, I noticed someone about twenty feet away, struggling to heave a large rock into the water below. When I looked closer, I realized who it was: Michael, the toughest kid on my Little League team, my partner in the greatest homeless man's porn heist our little suburb had ever seen, and the most fearless person I had ever known. I hadn't stayed in touch with Michael since those days; all I knew was that he'd been expelled from our high school in tenth grade after he'd gotten into an argument with a classmate, then grabbed the kid's bicycle, rode it two miles down to the cliffs above the Pacific, and hurled it into the sea.

"Hey," I yelled, walking toward him.

"Fuck you! I'm allowed to throw rocks, dickhead," he hollered back.

"No, it's Justin Halpern," I said.

"I know."

He set the large rock down onto the concrete and walked toward me. He was wearing a wife-beater and slacks, and had a collared shirt tied around his head like a bandana. His body had leaned out since our Little League days, but his face had hardened, and he looked as intimidating as ever.

"Is there still a magician in there?" he asked, pointing at the Bali Hai.

"I don't know. I couldn't get in. They said I'd already shown up and wouldn't let me back in."

"Ah, fuck, sorry. I used your name to get in."

He grabbed a joint out of his pocket and lit it up. I decided I should probably head out before the combination of Michael and drugs landed me in jail.

"All right, man. Well, good seeing you," I said, turning to walk back to my car.

"Can you find out if that magician is still in there?" he asked.

"Why?"

"He was doing some fucking dumb magic trick, trying to make this deck of cards disappear. So he's like, 'Does anybody know where my gay deck of cards are?' and I raised my hand and said, 'In your pussy.' Fuckin' guy had me thrown out."

Finding out whether the magician was still at the party seemed easy enough, and I felt a bit proud that Michael was asking me a favor, so I walked back to Mr. Bartess, who confirmed that the magician was still inside. Then I went back and told Michael, who was lying on the jagged rocks between the boardwalk and the ocean, polishing off his joint.

"I'm going back in there," Michael said, sitting up quickly. "If you come with me, I'll sneak you in."

"Uh . . . I don't know, dude. If they catch us, it wouldn't be good. I think I'm just gonna go home."

"Fine. I'll go by myself," he said without hesitation.

"What if they arrest you or something?" I asked, genuinely wondering whether Michael ever thought things through before he acted.

"Look. All I know is, that magician thinks I'm his bitch. And I'm not leaving tonight until I tell him he can eat a dick."

My gut told me just to leave; I didn't need this night to get any worse. But I thought about what leaving meant. I'd drive home, crawl into bed, turn off the lights, and that would be the end of prom—and, really, the end of high school. Maybe I hadn't had the kind of prom they made movies about, but sneaking into the after-party with Michael felt like giving myself one more chance.

"Okay. Let's do it," I said.

We approached the restaurant, walked around to the back, and waited for one of the kitchen staff to open the service door. When a heavy-set cook in a white smock came out carrying a huge bag of trash, we snuck past him into the kitchen, which was dark and empty. Beyond the dining room door, I could hear the sounds of a crowd.

"When we get in, we should just hang out in a corner or something for a bit, so no one notices us," I said.

"That sounds fuckin' dumb," Michael said. With that, he pushed through the kitchen doors into a room filled with makeshift blackjack tables and fake palm fronds. Michael headed straight toward the balding forty-year-old magician, who was surrounded by a dozen of my classmates, all staring at him like they were either on drugs or *really* into disappearing birds.

Michael pushed aside a skinny kid and planted himself in front of the magician.

"Hey, you fucking piece of shit!" Michael yelled.

The magician and all of the students surrounding him froze, staring at Michael, wondering what would come next.

"Eat my dick!" Michael yelled.

The magician's face turned bright red. He whirled to his right and, before his cape could catch up with his body, screamed for security.

Within seconds, two large men with black, puffy EVENT STAFF jackets stormed Michael from behind and grabbed him by the arms. Michael immediately went limp, forcing the guards to drag his lifeless body out of the restaurant as he shouted obscenities. Just as they pulled him through the doorway, he threw both his arms up in triumph and yelled, "Fuck everyone!"

I glanced around the room and saw that none of my friends were there. They'd probably already checked into hotel rooms somewhere. I was about to leave when I spotted Nicole by the ice-cream bar. She was wearing a long cream-colored dress that perfectly accented her olive skin. As I watched her shake sprinkles onto her soft serve, I realized that my prom night had really started going wrong two weeks before, when I'd wussed out on asking her. Here was my chance to redeem myself. Still reeling from Michael's scene, I suddenly realized: this could be my *Eat a dick!* moment. I strode up to Nicole with a sense of purpose I hadn't felt all night.

"Hi," I said, gently tapping her on the shoulder.

"Oh, hey!" she said, beaming and giving me a hug.

"How was your night?" I asked.

"Awesome. How was yours?"

"Pretty awesome. So, this is going to sound really weird, but I wanted to ask *you* to prom," I said.

As soon as I said it, I felt as if my stomach had dropped out of my pants.

"You did?"

"Yeah," I said, a bit more sheepishly.

"Why didn't you?"

"Because I thought you'd say no and then nobody else would want to go with me because they'd think they were my second choice. But I really should have just asked you, right?"

It felt good to tell her. Even more than that, my mind filled with fantasies about what her response might be. Even though she wasn't my official prom date, maybe we could hang out the rest of the night. Maybe we could even start dating. I had my mom's Oldsmobile Achieva for at least another hour, and it still had a half tank of gas. Maybe Nicole and I could actually get crazy after all.

"Awwww," she said sweetly, my heart rate picking up as she smiled at me. "I would have said no, though," she added.

"What?"

"I'm sorry. I'm just being honest. You're not really my type. I wouldn't have gone to prom with you."

Just then, a thin, handsome guy with a goatee came up behind her and wrapped his arms around her waist. He looked old enough to be in college.

"Ready?" he said softly into her ear.

Nicole nodded, then gave me another quick hug and left, her fingers entwined in her date's.

Nicole's rejection didn't sting quite as much as I expected, and the only reason I could figure was because for the first time that night, I had done exactly what I wanted to do.

You Are Good at Sit Down

In the fall of 1998 I began my freshman year at San Diego State University, which my dad commonly referred to as "Harvard, without all the smart people." Even though the campus was only eight miles from my parents' house and about a fifth of my high school graduating class was also heading to SDSU, I felt like it would be a new adventure and I was excited to begin.

"I'm pretty sure no one knew who I was in high school," I said to my best friend Dan, who was also going on to SDSU, as we drove to freshman orientation a few weeks before classes started.

"I dunno. I think people knew who you were," Dan said as he merged onto the 8 freeway. "I was telling this guy on my volleyball team that we were both going to State and he was like, 'Isn't he that guy who wears sweatpants to school sometimes?' "

"Ideally I'd like to be known as something other than that."

"Who gives a shit about high school? We're going to be in college now. Nobody knows us here. Girls want to party with crazy dudes. You could be the crazy party guy. Or I could be, and you could be that guy's friend."

The idea that I could entirely change all the things I didn't like about myself and wipe my slate clean was enticing. Unfortunately, I was going to have to try to do so while living at home, because, despite working all summer, I had less than five hundred dollars to my name when the fall rolled around.

My mom understood my plight and tried her best to offer up a solution.

"If you want to make love to a woman in the house, I promise we won't bother you," she said one night during dinner when I was a couple weeks into my first semester.

"Let me add an addendum to that. You find a woman that'll screw you with your mom next door, you run the fuck the other way," my dad said.

Despite my hopes of reinventing myself as a fearless social animal, I spent the first year of college the same way I had spent high school—hanging out with my high school friends and meeting practically no one new. When it came to partying, San Diego State seemed like the major leagues: it was as if every high school had sent its craziest party animals to compete in a tournament. When I did make it to a party, I usually found myself standing to the side, moving only when some incredibly drunk person stumbled toward me and said something like,

"I'm gonna pee here. Could you stand in front of me?" Whenever I was given the chance to melt into the walls, I did.

My friend Ryan, who also attended San Diego State, was similarly frustrated with his freshman year experience, so I was not entirely surprised when, midway through our second semester, he suggested that the two of us get out of Dodge for the summer. Ryan suggested we should take the money we had saved from our job cleaning boats all year and backpack through Europe.

"Everyone I know who's gone over there has partied with girls and had a bunch of sex," Ryan said as we drove home from class one day.

"How many people do you know that've gone over there?" I asked.

"Hmm. I guess I only know one guy. But that's what he said."

That was good enough for me. And I could think of no better travel companion than Ryan, whom I'd been friends with since I was five years old. He was a grade above me, so it wasn't until I started college, and found myself in a lot of classes with him, that we became really close. Lean and sinewy, with a mop of so-blonde-it's-white hair on top of his head, Ryan looks like a cross between a mad scientist and the winner of a surfing competition. He is easily the most positive human being I've ever met but also one of the strangest, as evidenced by the time he sat me down in high school and informed me, "There's a fifty-fifty chance the moon is actually an alien spaceship that's observing us." But he could be convincing—at least when it came to more earthly pleasures— and together we booked plane tickets for Europe, leaving in July and returning in early August, along with an unlimited EuroRail pass.

The night before we left, I excitedly stuffed my suitcase with as

many pairs of underwear and condoms as possible. I was still a virgin, but I was pretty sure Europe would put an end to that. I hadn't
been to another country since I was three years old, and I'd spent the
whole second semester of my freshman year waiting for this trip. It
was going to be the first real adventure of my life, although I stopped
referring to it as an "adventure" after my brother told me that was
"the pussiest thing I've ever heard someone say." Regardless, I could
barely contain my enthusiasm when my parents came into my bedroom as I was cramming a toothbrush into the tiny front pouch of my
oversized Jansport backpack.

"All right, real quick, couple things," my dad said, sitting down
on my desk chair. "You know how I get pissed off when we're driving around San Diego and some asshole in a rental car doesn't know
where the hell he's going?"

"Yeah," I said.

"Well, over there, you're the asshole in the rental. Be respectful
of people and their culture, okay? I don't want to pull you out of a
secret prison because you pissed on some sacred monument when
you were drunk."

"I'll have Ryan with me," I said.

"That guy's a minor head injury away from eating his own shit.
Not much of a case you're making."

"Call us every couple of weeks to let us know you're okay," my
mom said.

"I don't know if there's always going to be a phone around."

"You're not leading a fucking expedition to Antarctica. Find a
phone. Call," my dad insisted.

The next day Ryan and I flew from San Diego to London, via New York. After eighteen hours of traveling, just after sunrise, we dropped our packs in our crammed room in a dingy hostel near Trafalgar Square. We grabbed breakfast at a nearby pub, where Ryan studied his copy of *Let's Go Europe* like he was going to have to recite it for his Bar Mitzvah.

"Ibiza!" he said, looking up from the book like he'd uncovered a clue in a murder case.

"What's that?" I asked in between forkfuls of overcooked eggs.

"It's an island near Spain where I guess people just party twenty-four hours a day," he explained, as he scanned the book. "Whoa. It says there's a club on the island where two people just have sex in the middle of the dance floor the whole night," he added, continuing to read.

The whole reason I had come to Europe was to go to places like Ibiza, places where letting loose and getting crazy were my only option and I would be forced into the ring. I was in.

The next few days we toured London, seeing Buckingham Palace, the Tower Bridge, and finally getting into a heated argument with a Londoner after Ryan suggested that Big Ben should be called Medium Sized Ben, because "it's not even that big." After packing in as much sightseeing as we could, we took the Chunnel from London to Paris, where we spent a couple days rushing through museums and eating anything that had butter on it, and from Paris we headed to Switzerland for several days and then Florence.

When we arrived in Florence, it was a hundred and ten degrees. We checked into our hostel, which consisted of two large rooms packed with twenty bunk beds each, and two bathrooms total. Ryan and I walked through the narrow passageway between the beds, all the way to the back of the room, where the top bunks of two beds were open. On the bottom of Ryan's bunk lay a very thin Vietnamese man in his early twenties. Despite the oppressive heat, he was wearing a denim jacket, denim jeans, a blue T-shirt with Michael Jordan's face on it, and a pair of matching blue Chuck Taylor Converse shoes. Beads of sweat covered his forehead, dripping down his face as he lay there. Ryan reached his hand out and introduced himself.

"Hey, I'm Ry."

"Vietnam Joe," the man said, in a thick accent.

"Aren't you kinda hot in all that stuff, Joe?" Ryan asked.

"Large hot," Joe said, grabbing a tissue out of his jacket pocket and wiping his forehead.

"If you're worried about your jacket getting stolen, I have a lock on my bag—you can put it in there and it'll be fine," I said.

Joe had no reaction, so I pointed at his jacket, then at my bag and my lock.

"No," Joe said.

"I like Joe's style. Fuck it, it's hot, but he likes how he looks in his jacket. I understand that," Ryan said.

When we left the hostel a few minutes later to go to dinner, Joe walked out with us. He proceeded to follow us, two steps behind, all the way to a nearby restaurant whose menu we couldn't decipher but whose prices looked affordable.

"Do you want to have dinner with us, Joe?" I asked.

"Yes."

The three of us sat down at a table in the restaurant's air-conditioned interior, and Ryan and I learned quickly that Joe's English vocabulary was limited to about fifty words. Food was either "large delicious," "delicious," or "not delicious." Temperatures were either "large hot" or "not hot." Oddly, there was one full English sentence he could manage: "Second-year guard Ray Allen has a silky-smooth, NBA-ready game." When Joe saw how entertained we were by this, he showed us the Ray Allen basketball card that he kept in his wallet, which bore this very sentence. Since Ryan and I knew not one word of Vietnamese, we tried to communicate with Joe using the English words he knew, so he wouldn't feel left out.

After dinner, and over the next couple days, Joe joined me and Ryan as we explored Florence. He was up for any activity, especially if it involved going somewhere near to a leather goods shop. He loved leather, insisted on browsing through any store that sold it, and at one point purchased a pair of burgundy leather shorts, which he later tried on for us at the hostel before pronouncing them "unstoppable" (another word he'd found on the Ray Allen card). Joe was good-natured, a fun guy to have around, and he seemed to have traveled to Europe for the same reasons we had. A couple days after meeting him, the three of us sat down for lunch at a small café near our hostel and Ryan broke down our plan.

"Ibiza," Ryan said, pointing at a picture of one of the island's many nightclubs in a Spanish travel guidebook he'd bought that day.

"You, me, Ryan, Ibiza?" I said to Joe.

"Large hot?" Joe said, looking at the picture.

"Everywhere is large hot, Joe. There's a heat wave in Europe," Ryan responded.

Joe sat back for a moment thinking as he picked up his glass of ice water and ran it against his forehead.

"Large girls?" Joe asked.

"Oh, dude. Tons of large girls. This is why we're here, Joe. We've waited the whole trip to meet girls in Ibiza and start partying," Ryan said.

"Hmmmm," Joe said.

"Joe. You will like Ibiza. Silky-smooth guard Ray Allen and his NBA-ready game would like Ibiza."

Joe laughed. "Second-year guard Ray Allen has a silky-smooth, NBA-ready game."

"I think that's a yes," Ryan said to me.

The three of us walked to the train station and bought tickets for the following day to Barcelona, where we'd catch the ferry to Ibiza. We must have looked like one of those movies where three animals that would never get along in the wild join forces to find their way back home.

I figured the next couple days were going to be a total blackout, so I decided to give my parents a call that evening. After I chatted with my mom for a few minutes, she put my dad on the line.

"So, how's it going? You seeing some art and history or you too busy trying to slap your pecker against anything with a wet spot?"

"No, I saw some art. We spent like two hours in the Louvre."

"Nice. Two thousand years of priceless works of art and you bust through it in two hours. Eat shit, da Vinci," he said. "Where you heading next?"

"An island called Ibiza," I said.

"It's pronounced Ibitha," he replied.

"You've heard of it?"

"I hate to shit on your preconceived notions of me, but I'm pretty goddamn worldly."

"Well, that's where we're going," I said, looking at my watch to make sure I hadn't used up too much of my prepaid calling card.

"Feel free to tell me to piss off, but why in the hell are you going to some shit stain in the middle of the ocean?"

"It's supposed to be one big party, twenty-four hours a day."

"Sounds like the worst place on earth. Woulda thought you hated shit like that."

"Well, I don't," I said.

"Whatever floats your boat. Well, anyway, have fun and don't screw a woman if she's on drugs."

It's not often that a sane human being thinks, "I'll show my dad I can party," but that phrase reverberated in my head for the next couple hours.

The next day, Ryan, Joe, and I boarded a train to Barcelona. Our train car looked and smelled like it had once been used to transport slaughtered livestock. There was no air-conditioning on board, and each train car was filled with sweaty travelers. By the time we found seats, Joe had already broken into a full body sweat that was threatening to seep through his denim jacket.

Just before the train took off, a group of three girls in their late teens wearing summery dresses and carrying backpacks embroidered with the Mexican flag sat down in the row ahead of us. Joe looked at us, then the girls, then back at us. Then he gave us a thumbs-up.

"It's a super-long train ride. We should talk to these girls. Try and get them to go to Ibiza with us," Ry whispered.

"Totally," I whispered back.

"Maybe we wait until they get up to go to the bathroom or something, then start up a conversation. Ask them what the weirdest house they've ever seen is, or something," Ry said.

"I don't think that's a good opener," I whispered.

"What? Yes it is. It's not a yes-or-no question. They have to talk about the house and why it's weird, and that starts a conversation."

Before we could argue, Joe was tapping the girl in front of him on the shoulder. She turned around.

"Train large hot, yes?" Joe said to her.

"It is really hot. Our whole trip, everywhere has been hot," the girl said with a thick Spanish accent.

"Vietnam Joe," he said, sticking his hand out to shake.

"Abelena," she said, shaking his hand. "Where are you going to?"

"Hey, we're Joe's friends. You guys are from Mexico, huh? What's the weirdest house you've ever seen there?" Ryan interrupted.

"We're going to Ibiza," I quickly added.

"Fiesta," Joe said, smiling and nodding his head, causing all the girls to laugh.

"That's funny," Abelena said to Joe.

Within twenty minutes the three girls had turned around in their seats and were focusing intensely on Joe, who was showing them detailed pencil drawings of motorcycles he had sketched in a journal.

"For Joe," he said, pointing at one specific drawing of an aerodynamic-looking motorcycle.

"That is definitely the best one. I can see why you like it," Abelena said to him.

"Which one is for me?" her friend asked, smiling at Joe like he was a celebrity she had waited in line to meet.

Ryan turned to me in disbelief.

"Dude. I don't even know what's going on right now, but it is super awesome," Ryan said.

By the time we reached Barcelona, not only had Joe invited Abelena to sit next to him, where she now slept with her head on his shoulder, but he had gotten her travel companions warmed up to us. Ryan and I spent most of the ten-hour ride chatting with Eloisa and Anetta, who, we learned, were freshmen in college and lived in Mexico City. The weirdest house they'd ever seen, they told us, was a house in Tijuana that looked like a giant naked woman. At about four in the morning, when almost everyone else on the train was sleeping, I asked Eloisa if she and her friends wanted to come to Ibiza with us. She said yes.

The next morning, my eyes opened just as we were pulling into the Barcelona train station. Ryan, Joe, the three girls, and I grabbed our packs and walked down to the ferry building in the Barcelona harbor to purchase our tickets for a ship leaving that night. Just as we were about to get in line, Joe pulled Ryan and me aside.

"I no Ibiza," Joe said.

"What? Do you need to borrow money?" I asked, grabbing my wallet and showing him a few Euros to make my point.

"No. Money I own."

"Then what's the problem?" Ryan asked.

Abelena approached with her bag.

"Joe and I are going to go to San Sebastián together. It was very nice meeting you guys," she said. Then she walked back to her friends, exchanged a few sentences in Spanish with them, and hugged them good-bye.

"Wow," Ryan said.

"Yes," Joe said.

"Well, it was really great meeting you, Joe," I said.

"Yes. I want fun time for Justin. Fun time for Ryan," he replied.

"Thanks, man."

"I own sad," he added.

"We own it, too, man," I said.

I gave Joe my e-mail address. Then Ryan and I watched as he and Abelena walked out of the ferry station together.

After bumming around on the beach all day, Ryan, Eloisa, Anetta, and I boarded a dilapidated ship whose rusted exterior and cracked floorboards made it look like it should have been setting sail for Ellis Island in the summer of 1925. As we pulled away from the harbor, Ryan and I stood out on the bow.

"This is it, dude. We're going to the party capital of the world. We have girls with us. Stuff is going to get crazy, and we have to get crazy with it. No excuses," Ryan said.

"Totally," I agreed.

We didn't have enough money for a room on board, so the four of us slept in lounge chairs on the observation deck. Thirteen hours later, the sun smacked us across the face, waking us up just as we were approaching the island. Ibiza looked to be a series of hills, covered in small white Mediterranean homes, plunging down to a sandy beach lined with grand resorts and the turquoise ocean below. When we disembarked from the boat, we realized we had no idea where to go. All the other tourists grabbed taxis and drove off toward the resorts, but we couldn't afford those rates, and we weren't about to waste money on a cab. The streets were deserted and it was horror-movie quiet. We shrugged our shoulders, chose a direction almost at random, and started walking down a narrow street when suddenly a voice from behind us said, "You guys lost?"

Standing behind us was a bronzed American man in his late twenties, wearing baggy white pants, a pair of bright red shoes covered in sparkles, an electric-blue short-sleeve T-shirt that seemed to be made of Lycra, and a pair of Oakley-style sunglasses with fluorescent yellow lenses. He reminded me of an animal you'd see in a nature special about how the most dangerous species in the Amazon use their colorful markings as a warning to other animals.

"I can show you around. I need to walk off this E. I'm rolling balls so fucking hard right now," he said, running his hands through his spiked hair, then popping his pinkie in his mouth and tugging on his cheek like a fish that'd been hooked.

With no real idea where we were going, we took him up on his offer, and headed off in the exact opposite direction from the one we'd chosen. As we walked, he explained that he lived on the island and worked as a promoter for a few different clubs.

"It's my job to make sure the party is super-hot. If it's not hot enough, I make it hotter," he said as we walked down the boardwalk.

"So what's the hottest party to go to in Ibiza?" Ryan asked.

"You can't handle that party. If you touched that party, it would burn you."

"Okay. Well, what about the second hottest party?" I asked.

"Still too hot for you," he said.

"Just tell us a party that's appropriately hot for us," Ryan snapped.

He looked us up and down. "Club Pacha," he said.

He led us to a hostel that sat at the end of a small alley, above an auto shop, and was on his way.

As soon as we got into our tiny single room, Eloisa and Anetta went into the bathroom together and threw on skirts and bikini tops. Then the four of us headed down to the beach. We spent the day lounging on the sand in front of a hotel and swigging from a small bottle of vodka we'd brought with us from Barcelona. Everything was going just as I'd hoped; even things I was normally self-conscious about seemed unimportant.

"So, I kinda have weird chest hair," I said, as I removed my shirt.

"I like it. It looks like an eagle that's grabbing another eagle," Anetta said.

"Fuck yeah. It totally looks like a crazy eagle fight," Ryan chimed in.

*   *   *

We knew we weren't going to be able to afford drinks at the club, so that evening Ryan and I walked to a nearby liquor store, bought a couple dozen airplane-sized bottles of Skyy Vodka, Captain Morgan's, and Jack Daniels, and stuffed them in our pants pockets so that it looked like we were wearing football pads. By the time our taxi arrived at Pacha, the four of us had downed several bottles each and my tongue was starting to feel numb. Before us was a big white building, with two large palm trees flanking the entrance and a wash of purple floodlights over the whole facade.

As other people gathered in front of the club, though, we started feeling out of place. Ryan and I were both wearing khaki slacks and I was wearing New Balance sneakers, whereas almost everyone around us was dressed in all-white clothing so skin-tight it looked like they were heading to a speed-skating competition. Standing next to them, I looked like an old man on the way to his grandson's third-grade play.

"Man. Everyone looks like they're from the future," Ryan said.

We pushed past the front door and into a cavernous open room where the techno music's pulsing bass smacked me in the face and vibrated through my body. The walls were twenty feet high and draped in white fabric; all around us, purple and white spotlights chased each other fast enough to give you motion sickness. In the middle of the room was a concrete dance floor packed with hundreds of sweaty bodies writhing around like they were going through heroin withdrawal. Sitting above the dancers in the DJ booth was a middle-aged bald man wearing a cape who periodically grabbed a strobe light and flashed it over the crowd. Even though we were standing on the outskirts of the dance floor, arms and legs flailed wildly and knocked into us every few seconds.

"Man, people dance really weird here," I shouted as loud as I could, so that Ryan could hear me over the music.

"Come outside for a sec," Ryan yelled back at me, then held his hand up to Eloisa's ear and said something to her.

We walked away from the dance floor and up some stairs to a rooftop lounge where the music was quieter. A group of young people were smoking cigarettes in a huddle; in a booth nearby sat an obese man with a hairline that started at his eyebrows, with one incredibly attractive woman on his lap and two others on either side of him.

"We can't start making excuses not to party," Ryan said, insistently.

"What are you talking about? I'm here. I'm ready to party."

"No. You just said, 'People dance really weird here,' " he replied.

"They do. I'm just making an observation. Here's another one: That fat guy has a lot of hot girls around him. Just an observation," I said.

"That fat guy is partying. You stand around talking about how weird people are, and you'll end up doing that the whole night. I do it, too. But we can't do that shit," Ryan said, his eyes growing wilder as he talked.

"What are you, my coach? I don't need you to give me a speech, dude."

"Yes, you do! Because I spent *all my money* to come to this place, dude. Did you know I was saving up to buy a dune buggy? But I didn't buy one. Instead I came here. To party."

"Why were you saving up to buy a dune buggy? Where would you even ride that?"

"I was gonna ride it to school or something. I don't know. It doesn't matter because I can't buy one now. But what I *can* do is fucking party, in the partiest party place in the world. Vietnam Joe is off somewhere in Spain and he speaks like two words of English and he's making sweet love to women and shit."

Ryan removed three minibottles of vodka from his pockets and unscrewed their caps. "Let's do this," he said, then tilted his head back and poured all three down his throat one after the other. I took out three bottles of Captain Morgan's and did the same, fighting the urge to throw them back up.

"Also, everyone here seems like they're into rich guys. So, if anyone asks you, I'm telling people my dad invented the calculator watch, and my name is Brian Waters," he said as he tossed the empty bottles into a trash can. "Who are you?" he asked.

"Hmm. I don't know."

"I like the name Robert C. Manufas. I mean, it's your call, but I'm just saying I like that one."

"How about this: I'm Robert C. Manufas and I own an Internet company that helps people find tax loopholes?"

"Hell, yeah," he said giving me a high five.

We each downed one more tiny bottle of liquor and strode confidently back into the club. Ryan grabbed Eloisa, who was standing where we'd left her, and walked out onto the dance floor. I spotted Anetta out on the floor, making out with a tall guy in a white jumpsuit with the zipper opened down to his belly button, revealing his shaved chest. I stood on the periphery of the dance floor for a few moments. I have never been what you would call "a good dancer." I have one move: reaching my arms out wide, leaning back, and lurching my chest forward to the rhythm of the music, like a guy being shot repeatedly in the back. But that night, I pushed that move to its absolute limits.

The only way I could even keep track of time passing was that every so often a giant cloud of freezing vapor would blast from the corner of the room, making it impossible to see your hand in front of your face for a few seconds. Ryan drank all of his tiny bottles of liquor, and most of mine, and spent what felt like several hours carrying Eloisa on his shoulders and challenging other couples to chicken fights until security insisted he stop. I danced till seven in the morning with anyone who made the mistake of making eye contact with me.

Toward the end of the night, I was dancing with a tall, rangy blond woman who looked like she was in her late twenties. After an extended grinding session, she pulled me outside onto the upstairs balcony, where I noticed that the sky was becoming light.

"You're fucking intense," she said, then pounded an entire bottle of water, most of which ran down her chin and chest and onto her white tank top.

"Just dancing," I replied.

"What's your name?" she asked.

"Robert C. Manufas," I said, sticking to my script, then realizing no one ever says his full name and middle initial when answering that question.

"Do you have any E on you?" she asked.

"Ecstasy? No."

"Shit. Let's do shots of 151."

And that was the last thing I remembered.

The next day, at five P.M., I woke up in a bunk bed in our hostel. Ryan was sleeping facedown on the floor in just his underwear, the rest of his clothes balled up beneath his head like a pillow. Eloisa and Anetta were spooning each other in bed across the room. Ryan rolled over and looked at me.

"I think I blacked out," I said with a hoarse voice.

"Do you remember going out into the middle of the dance floor and challenging people to dance battles?" he asked, rubbing his eyes slowly.

"No. How did I do?"

"Mostly people just yelled at you. Then you stole a knife from the bartender and cut your sleeves off. Then the bartender asked for it back and you started making body builder poses and then ran away. So that was pretty awesome."

I smiled in victory and then realized I felt worse than I'd ever felt in my life. I sat up—a little too quickly, I guess, because I immediately projectile-vomited into an empty bag of chips. I went to wipe my mouth on my missing shirtsleeves, and ended up rubbing my puke onto my bare biceps.

"What do we do now?" I asked Ryan between sips of a water bottle I found next to me.

Ryan handed me a rolled-up piece of toilet paper, then took a moment to recover from the effort. Between deep breaths, he said, "We do it again."

And we did. The next night was almost identical. The only differences were, the club we went to was called Amnesia, which threw a "Purple Party" instead of a white one; my fake name was Peter Schlesinger and I sold yachts; I made out with a strange woman who asked me for cocaine instead of ecstasy; and I woke up the next morning feeling even worse than I had the morning before. Also, my underwear was on over my pants.

With two full nights in Ibiza under our belts, the four of us checked out of our hostel and boarded a boat back to Barcelona. I felt a sense of accomplishment. I had gone to Europe in hopes of becoming someone I was never able to be back home, and I was sure that, if I could be more like the guy I'd been for the past two days, my life would be infinitely better. I also felt really bloated. My stomach was hard to the touch; it looked like I was in my second trimester. I was exhausted, so I went inside the main cabin of the ship and plopped myself down in one of the couple hundred seats, shut my eyes, and fell asleep.

About four hours later my eyes shot open. It felt like I'd swallowed a rat that was now trying to claw its way up through my intestines to freedom. I tried to go back to sleep but couldn't; instead I ended up just sitting awake, slumped over in my chair, until we finally arrived at Barcelona nine hours later, just as the sun came up. When I tried explaining my agony to Ryan, who is not a "believer" in traditional medicine, he offered a theory of his own: "I bet you it's because of the frequencies in this ocean. Your cells probably aren't used to these frequencies."

"I don't think that's it," I replied, weakly.

I tried ignoring the pain, and I made it to the train station, where we boarded our train for Madrid. By the time we reached our hostel there a few hours later, though, I could barely stand up. The room we got for the night was windowless and felt at least fifteen degrees hotter than the temperature outside, which was well over a hundred. I collapsed on the bed closest to the door and curled into the fetal position in hopes I'd feel better, but as I moved my legs toward my chin I felt a stabbing pain shoot through my stomach and up into my chest.

"Ry, I need to go to the emergency room," I moaned.

"I think you're gonna be okay. You're away from the ocean now and its weird frequencies," he replied.

"Ry. I need to go to the emergency room right now, man."

Ryan nodded and gingerly lifted me out of bed. I slung one arm around him as he helped me downstairs and out onto the street, where we hailed a cab. About ten minutes later I was sitting in the waiting area of an emergency room when a nurse approached us and said something in Spanish that neither Ryan or I could understand.

"What is hurt?" she finally sputtered in broken English.

"I think the frequencies of the ocean have messed with his cells," Ryan said.

"My stomach hurts," I said.

"Point where," she said.

I gestured toward my entire stomach area and she nodded. Five minutes later she led me to a private room, where she started an IV in my left arm. Twenty minutes later I was standing in front of an X-ray machine.

The X-ray technician rattled off some directions in Spanish and I figured out from the key words that he wanted me to take off my clothes. Then I realized from the look on his face that at no point had he asked me to take off my underwear. I pulled them back up as quickly as I could, which in my pathetic condition wasn't very quickly at all. After he snapped a couple X-rays, I waited with Ryan until the nurse brought us into a small office where the doctor, a young woman in scrubs and a white lab coat, sat behind a desk, a set of X-rays spread out in front of her.

"*No hables español, si?*" she said.

"Not really," I said.

"Okay. I try explain in English," she replied as she held up an X-ray in front of us.

"Your stomach is very mad. It do not work. Here," she said, pointing to two dark areas under my ribcage. "This is, ah . . ." she added, then turned to the nurse and rattled off a question in Spanish.

The nurse picked it up where the doctor had left off. "Ah, I know this is not most correct but for understand—too much poo poo and fart," she said, pointing at the dark spots on the X-ray.

"That was the most awesome diagnosis I've ever heard in my life," Ryan said.

"Thank you," the nurse said without a hint of humor.

"What does that mean?" I asked.

"You got too many poo poos and farts in your stomach, dude. That's pretty clear," Ryan said, laughing.

"Have you eat drugs?" the doctor asked.

"No. Not at all."

"Alcohol?"

"Yes. A lot."

"We went to Ibiza," Ryan interjected.

The nurse and the doctor exchanged brief but satisfied smirks, as if they'd been placing bets on Ibiza.

"Okay, Justin," the doctor continued. "Some people, they are very good at alcohol, and they go to many discos, and it is okay. Some people, they are very bad at alcohol, and it is not good for them discos, and they are good at sitting. You are good at sit down."

She went on to tell me that, because of the drastic change in my lifestyle over the past forty-eight hours, my stomach had reacted violently and basically stopped working. Constipation and a buildup of gas were causing all the pain. She said I wouldn't really be able to walk around for the next few days, then handed me a prescription to alleviate the blockage and pain. I thanked her profusely and we left the emergency room and hobbled next door to the pharmacy.

As I rifled around in my wallet, preparing to pay the bill, I noticed my prepaid calling card and remembered that I owed my parents a call. After settling up, Ryan and I took a cab back to our hostel room where, exhausted, I sat down and dialed my parents' number. The phone picked up after one ring.

"It's four thirty in the fucking morning," my dad said.

"Oh, sorry, I forgot."

"Well who in the hell is this?"

"It's Justin, Dad."

"Justin? You sound like shit run over, son."

"Yeah, I'm not feeling well."

"Not feeling well how?" he said, his voice quickening with concern.

"Okay, well, don't tell Mom because she'll freak out, and I'm gonna be fine, but I just had to go to the emergency room."

"Aw, hell. For what?"

I explained everything I'd done in the past couple days: Ibiza, the minibottles of booze, the stomach pains, the X-rays, right down to the prescription I'd just been given. He listened quietly until I was finished.

"Can I make a suggestion?" he asked.

"Sure."

"Maybe next time you're thinking about getting shithouse drunk all night, you don't."

"Dad, I barely ever drink."

"Yeah, that's my point. You can't hold your liquor for shit. So maybe drinking a whole bunch of it and shaking your ass ain't your thing."

"We were just having a good time and trying to meet people, you know?"

"Well, you don't need to get shithoused and go to Europe to do that. You're over six feet tall and your mom says you're funny. I'd say run with those two things and see where it gets you."

We said good-bye just as my calling card was about to run out of minutes. Then I sat down on my bed, and, for what felt like the first time in days, I fell asleep.

A week later, Ryan and I were in Charles de Gaulle Airport in Paris, waiting to board our flight back home. My stomach was feeling infinitely better, although I was still relatively weak and couldn't walk more than a few blocks without having to sit down. We had an hour before our flight took off, so I decided to check my e-mail at an Internet kiosk in the terminal. At the top of my inbox was an e-mail from Vietnam Joe:

> Justin, I hope you have a great trip. I am using Vietnamese to English translation, so I apologize if there is incorrect grammar. I had a great time and met many very attractive women. I am on a good streak that I want to say that meeting you and Ryan and I think you are very great man. You must know a lot of attractive women. I hope to go out with you all one day when I came to the United States. I want to meet the women you know. I will not steal from you. Oh no I can not promise!
>
> *Joe*

A Man Takes His Shots and Then He Scrubs the Shit out of Some Dishes

Between the ages of sixteen and nineteen, each of my friends lost his virginity. One by one they fell, until finally, at the age of twenty, my friend Jeff and I were the only virgins left. I was in my second year of college and lived in a run-down five-bedroom house in Pacific Beach, San Diego, with Jeff and three other close friends. The morning after a party we threw celebrating the end of the first semester, I stumbled out of my bedroom and found my roommates hanging out in the grease-stained kitchen.

"Any milk left?" I asked, hoping to drown my hangover with Cinnamon Toast Crunch.

"Jeff had sex last night," my friend Dan said.

I froze.

Maybe he's joking, I thought. I looked at Jeff, who was standing in the corner of the room sipping a Gatorade with the swagger of someone who had won seven Super Bowls, and knew it was no joke.

"Jeff had sex? *Jeff?*" I said, in disbelief.

"Well, fuck you too, dude," Jeff replied.

"Sorry, I'm just surprised. I'm happy for you," I said.

I was not happy for him. Imagine if you and a friend were stranded on a desert island for the last five years. Then one day you wake up and saw your friend on a raft in the ocean, paddling toward a rescue ship. Then, as you scream, "Come back! Don't leave me!," your friend laughs and waves at you, then keeps paddling, without even looking back. That is exactly how I felt in that moment. It didn't seem that terrible to be a virgin when I wasn't the only one. Now I was the only member left in the club, and it was awful.

I never felt pressure from my friends to have sex. Nobody was getting laid that regularly, and even Dan, who probably had more sex than any of my other friends, rarely talked about it, for a reason he put rather eloquently: "I play tennis every once in a while, but I don't brag about it because I suck at it." But now that Jeff had had sex, I couldn't help but feel like they had stepped into manhood and I was on the outside looking in.

It wasn't like I hadn't been trying. It's not like I had some special being-awesome-with-the-ladies gear that I just hadn't chosen to shift into. I'd always been terrified of talking to women and usually just avoided it. When I headed to college, I tried to relax and not obsess over having sex, hoping it would just happen.

It didn't.

A couple months later, I finished my second year at San Diego State. During my sophomore year, I had played on the baseball team and spent fifty-plus hours a week practicing, playing, attending classes, and studying. That didn't leave much time for a job, so when summer rolled around, I had to make all the money I'd need for the year. On the first day of summer break, Dan and I drove around in his Mazda putting in applications at every restaurant, retail store, and hotel we could find. As we drove home from the last hotel just before sunset, we stopped at a stoplight near the beach. Directly in front of us, hanging from a blank storefront in a strip mall, was a giant banner:

GRAND OPENING

HOOTERS

NOW HIRING

"That'd be funny, if we applied to a Hooters," Dan said as the light turned green.

We drove along quietly for a few moments.

"We should apply there," I said.

"Yeah, that's a good idea," Dan said, suddenly turning the wheel hard and making a screeching U-turn in the middle of the street.

We parked out in front of the banner and went inside. The restaurant was still being built, so the inside was filled with construction workers and raw materials. In the corner were two men sitting at a desk: a big Korean man in his twenties, and a five-foot-tall, grizzled white guy in his midforties wearing a Hooters T-shirt and hat. He looked like the kind of guy who, if he hadn't killed a man himself, at least must have buried a body somewhere along the way. We approached them tentatively.

"Hi, are you guys taking applications?" I said.

"No. We just like to put a big-ass sign out front for shits and giggles and then sit around and talk to every dipshit that walks in here," the little man said in a raspy voice that suggested he'd been smoking since birth.

Dan and I stood silently for a moment, unsure if we were supposed to laugh.

"I'm busting your balls. Here's an application. I assume you're applying to be a cook. I'm Bob. This is Song Su," he added, pointing to his colleague.

Dan and I introduced ourselves, filled out the applications, and left.

For the next few days we continued to hunt for jobs, but later that week I got a call from Song Su.

"You guys got the job. Tell your tall friend that's pretty like a girl so I don't have to make two calls. Orientation is Monday," he said.

"That's awesome! Thank you!" I said.

"Don't get excited. The job sucks and you make minimum wage. I think. I can't remember. Whatever it is, it's terrible pay. See you Monday," he replied.

I didn't care how terrible the pay was going to be. I was going to be surrounded by women eight hours a day, five days a week. For the entire summer. I would literally be forced to talk to them. Maybe, just maybe, I was going to have sex.

A couple days later, I sat alongside Dan and eight other guys in two rows of chairs in a room at the back of the recently finished Hooters, covered in fake street signs and orange, as Song Su and Bob stood before us. Bob wore a mesh tank top and sported a mustache that would make any 1970s baseball player proud. He slowly puffed at a cigarette as he addressed the male members of his newly assembled staff.

"I know what you're all thinking. You're going to get some stank on your dick with one of these waitresses, that's why you took the job."

" 'Cause the job sucks," Song Su added.

"Yep. Job sucks," Bob nodded.

"Well, let me be the first to tell you," Bob continued. "That's probably going to happen. You're probably gonna nail one of them. I nailed one. Then I married her," he said.

"Whoa, no way," said a guy in the front row.

"Yes way, shithead. I took one down. Married her. She had my babies, the whole deal. Anyway, just do your work and don't piss me off, and you'll have a good time," Bob said, before spitting on the ground.

After his speech, he gave us a tour of the kitchen and the walk-in freezer, which he said was "an awesome place to get a hand job if you're not in the middle of a dinner rush." He finished up the tour by handing us black T-shirts with the Hooters logo emblazoned on the front. Then he welcomed us to the Hooters family, which transitioned into a bizarre tangent about his time in the military, where he warned us about "the kind of scum that fuck a man's wife when he's overseas in the shit."

As we drove out of the parking lot an hour and a half later, Dan made a comment that was hard to ignore: "Dude. I don't want to put any extra pressure on you, 'cause I know you're all weird about this virginity shit. But if that Bob guy can have sex with a Hooters girl, you have to be able to."

I agreed. I could barely contain my excitement. Sex had seemed so elusive, but now I felt like I was mere days away.

Two days later, Dan and I walked into Hooters for our first shift wearing our tan aprons and Hooters hats. We realized two things really quickly: 1) Song Su wasn't lying: the job definitely sucked; 2) the majority of the girls working there had major emotional problems. And not cries-too-much emotional problems; more like stabs-her-boyfriend-with-a-steak-knife-then-falls-into-a-corner-and-starts-whispering-to-herself emotional problems. Even if I knew how to talk to women like that, or wanted to—neither of which I did—the work day was so jam-packed with cleaning, scrubbing, wing-battering, and Dumpster-emptying that I didn't even have a chance.

One day I was washing dishes in the back when Bob poked his head in. "Skippy," he said. (Bob never remembered anyone's name. Nor did he bother to cover up this fact.) "Skippy, today is not your day. I'm going to tell you a story. Guy walks into a Hooters, gets drunk, pukes his fucking guts out up on the balcony. You clean it up, and afterward I buy you a beer and tell you you're a swell guy. The end. What do you think?"

"I hate that story, Bob," I said.

"Maybe it was in the telling," he said, handing me a mop and a bucket in tow. Even though the balcony stood fifty feet from the ocean, the stench of vomit overpowered the smell of the sea. I had found the mess and started scrubbing when I heard a woman's voice.

"I am super sorry about that. I probably shouldn't have kept serving him beers," she said.

I turned and saw that the voice belonged to a waitress named Sarah. She was tall and thin, with short blond hair, and her breasts were tucked into her Hooters uniform in a way that created a shelf below her chin that she could probably set her car keys on if she needed free hands. She had been fairly quiet in the month that I had worked there; my only interaction with her had been a week before, when she asked me if we were out of baked beans. But she did so politely and with a pretty smile.

"It's no big deal," I said, suddenly realizing how impossible it was to look cool while cleaning up vomit.

"I'll buy you a beer afterward. Actually, I have a six-pack in my car. We can drink them at the beach if you get off soon," she said.

After Sarah went back to work, I ran downstairs to Dan, who was up to his elbows in batter, lathering up raw chicken wings.

"Guess who asked me to drink beers with her after work?" I asked.

"I don't know. But Bob just handed me my paycheck. Eighty-three hours, after taxes, guess how much? Two hundred and forty-two dollars. For eighty-three fucking hours, dude. I almost cried. I seriously almost cried. I hate this fucking job. I blame you," he said, pulling a chicken wing out of the batter and hurling it against the wall.

"Are you still mad, or can I talk now?" I asked.

"I'm done. So which girl asked you to have beers?"

"Guess."

"I don't know. Sarah?"

"How'd you know that?"

" 'Cause they're all named Sarah."

I described which Sarah I meant, and how the conversation had gone down, as he battered the wings.

"Well, I'm actually not able to be happy right now, but if I were, I'd be happy for you," he said.

I couldn't wait for work to end. I was so excited that I didn't even mind it when Bob made me clean the Dumpster outside filled with rancid chicken wings.

Around midnight, after I finished cleaning out the oil in the fryers, Sarah and I made our way down to her Honda Civic and grabbed the six cans of warm Natty Ice she had rolling around in her backseat. We sat on the cement wall of the boardwalk looking out at the ocean and cracked the beers open and began drinking. I smelled like raw chicken, flour, and vomit. After a few moments of silence, though, I began to panic: here I was again, sitting next to a woman, with no idea how to talk to her.

"That guy really threw up everywhere," I said as an opener.

"Yeah, that was really gross. I'd rather not talk about it," she replied.

"Totally," I said.

I decided my only chance at this going well was to stop talking and just go in for a kiss. So I did—until I realized she had a mouthful of beer, and my surprise kiss caused her to cough it up in my face.

"Oh my God, I'm really, really sorry," I said, patting her on the back as she coughed.

"Wrong pipe," she said between coughs. Finally she caught her breath. "Let me finish a couple more beers and then we'll make out, okay?"

She did, and we did. And then we did the same thing the next night, and the night after that. Then make-outs at night turned into hang-outs during the day, and before I knew it we'd been hanging out and making out for about a month. I'd made out with a few girls before her, but I'd never had a consistent make-out partner. I felt like an athlete in the midst of a winning streak; I wasn't sure why everything was working, but it was and I didn't want to screw it up.

"You think she thinks you're her boyfriend?" asked Dan one day at work while we cleaned the stainless-steel prep station in the back of the kitchen.

"I'm not sure. We just kind of only make out, and rent movies and watch them and don't really talk a bunch. I like her, though. She's cool," I said.

"You've been hanging out with her a lot, dude. If you like her, you should just ask her if she's your girlfriend, because if she is, you guys should be having sex, not making out," Dan said.

"Get some stank on your hang low," Bob yelled out from the manager's office, where, evidently, he'd been eavesdropping.

Dan was right. I did like Sarah. She was quiet but very sweet and cute, and we had the same taste in rental movies. And if I liked her, and she liked me, why weren't we having sex?

That night, when I was at Sarah's little one-bedroom stucco apartment in Rancho Bernardo, we were making out on her fake leather couch the way we usually did. At one point she got up to get a glass of water and I followed her to the kitchen.

"This is a super-weird question to ask, but do you tell people I'm your boyfriend?" I asked.

She lit up a cigarette and took a few puffs.

"No one has really asked me. But, I mean, I like hanging out with you, so I guess you kind of are," she said. "We haven't had sex, though," she added.

"Yeah, that's why I thought maybe we weren't," I said.

"Well, we can. I just hadn't 'cause we'd just been hanging out for a couple weeks, and then I've been on my period. But why don't you rent a movie and come over Friday night?"

I could barely sleep the next two nights, I was so excited. I'd spent most of my adolescence fantasizing about sex, and now it was about to happen. I thought about how it might go down. Maybe I'd take off her bra with one hand while saying something cool, but not douchey. Then we'd turn off a couple lights, and go at it for forty-five minutes to an hour, and I'd give her two to three orgasms. The anticipation was killing me. I had struggled with women my whole life; I'd never been comfortable in my own skin, never felt like a man. I just felt like a boy who got older. And, while I didn't know what the steps were to start to feel like a man, I was sure that having sex must be one of them.

The next day I bounded into work, tossed on my apron, and found Dan cutting limes in the kitchen.

"You didn't come home last night. You guys do it?" Dan asked.

"No. But she says I'm her boyfriend, and the only reason we haven't done it is because she's on her period," I said proudly.

"That's why God made the butthole, my friend. One door closes, the other one opens," Bob chimed in from a few feet away.

That Friday evening, a couple hours before my shift ended, Bob came into the kitchen to let me off early for the night.

"Before you go, though," he said, "your skinny buddy said you're about to get your cherry popped."

I looked angrily behind Bob and spotted Dan trying to hide a smile as he scrubbed the mop sink.

"Let me tell you something," Bob said earnestly as he put his hand on my shoulder. "I lost my virginity when I was fourteen, on mushrooms, to a two-hundred-pound woman who ran the Laundromat by my dad's house. Then I spent the next two hours taking a dump in her toilet."

"Okay."

"I'm glad I got a chance to tell you that," he said, then patted me on the back.

I got in my car and drove to the Blockbuster near my apartment, where I rented a copy of *A Few Good Men*. Sarah had never seen it, and it was one of my favorite movies.

As I drove over to Sarah's, I was filled with nerves, excitement, and a little bit of nausea. It was the same feeling I'd had when I got up with the bases loaded in the championship game of my last year of Little League. That ended with me getting hit in the stomach with a fastball and puking on home plate. I could only hope that this would end differently.

I got to her apartment shortly before midnight, with a DVD, twelve condoms, and an entire chocolate cake, which seemed like a good idea when I was in the drugstore checkout line, but immediately felt ridiculous as I carried it through Sarah's front door.

We had a couple beers on her couch, then crawled into her double bed and put on *A Few Good Men*. Usually, about five minutes into a movie we would start making out and one of us would pause the film. This time, though, I hesitated to make the first move, because for so long the first move had been the only move. Now there was supposed to be a second move: doing it.

Twenty minutes of the movie went by, then forty, and I still hadn't done anything. Finally I started kissing Sarah's neck, then lifted up her shirt. I couldn't figure out how to unhook her bra, so I pulled it down and awkwardly put my mouth on her boob.

"What are you doing?" Sarah asked.

I popped my head up.

"What?" I asked.

"What are you doing?" she asked again.

"Kissing your boob?"

"Well, it's just—they're talking about whether or not Jack Nicholson ordered the code red on that guy," she said, pointing at the TV screen.

I grabbed the remote and pushed pause.

"There you go. You won't miss it," I said.

She grabbed the remote and unpaused the movie.

"I want to see if he ordered the code red," she snapped.

"He ordered the code red."

"I don't think he did."

"Of course he did. That's what the whole movie is about. I've seen the movie."

"Geez, well, thanks for ruining it for me!"

"Ruining it for you? They tell you forty-five minutes into the movie that he ordered the code red. The rest of the movie is just about whether or not Tom Cruise can get him to *say* he ordered the code red."

"Don't tell me what the movie's about! I know what it's about!"

By now, of course, I had absolutely destroyed any mood there was to begin with, and hurt her feelings in the process. I needed to think of something fast.

"I'm sorry. Do you want some cake?" I asked.

"What?"

"Let's just watch the movie. I promise I didn't ruin it for you," I said.

"Sorry, I'm just into the movie. Why don't we just have sex right now? That way we can watch the movie afterward and not have to worry about having sex," she said.

Now that I'm older, it seems like a pretty obvious sign that your relationship isn't going well if your partner asks you to get sex out of the way so she can finish a movie. At the time, though, it sounded like a perfectly reasonable request and I jumped at her offer.

I pressed pause again, pulled out a condom, and started to open it—first with my hands, then with my teeth, then, finally and frantically, with both teeth and hands, which proved successful. Then I reached over and flipped off the lights, and for about a minute and thirty seconds we had sex. In all the thousands of sexual fantasies I'd had, I only concerned myself with making exactly one person happy: me. But as I rolled around on top of her, like a zombie trying to maul a sleeping camper in a horror film, I fully realized all the pressures that come with having sex with someone. I was supposed to try to make it as good for her as it was for me. I had responsibilities. And it soon became evident—as soon as I realized it would be over very quickly— that I didn't know what it would take to make things enjoyable for her. Before that night, when I'd heard someone say their first time was disappointing, it had always rubbed me the wrong way, like hearing a millionaire tell you their life is too complicated. But now that I'd had sex, I *was* disappointed—because I had sucked so badly at it. There was nothing romantic about it.

After I finished, I collapsed on top of her. She tilted her body and I slid off her. She went to the bathroom, then got back in bed and hit the play button on the remote. I was asleep before Jack Nicholson yelled "YOU CAN'T HANDLE THE TRUTH!"

The next morning, Sarah left early to pick up her sister from the airport; when I woke up she had already gone. I drove back to my apartment, unsure whether what had happened could be considered a success. When I walked in, Dan was having breakfast.

"You do it?" he asked as soon as I walked in.

"I did it," I said.

"Let me guess how long. Five minutes?"

"Divided by two . . . and then minus another minute, I think."

"Look who just became a man!" he said, laughing.

A couple days later, Sarah called me while I was at work. Bob called me into his office and handed me the phone.

"I don't like personal calls, Skippy," he said.

"Sorry, I'll make it quick," I said, and picked up the phone.

"What's up?" I said into the receiver.

What was up was, she thought we should break up.

"So, you're really nice, but I just don't think I'm going to work at Hooters anymore, and it'll be hard for us to see each other and stuff," she said.

"Okay," I said, trying not to reveal my hurt feelings.

"Okay. Sorry. Could you put Bob back on? I want to tell him where to send my last check."

I handed Bob the phone.

"She needs to talk to you," I said.

I turned to walk away.

"Hey," Bob said, stopping me. He held his hand over the receiver. "Just make sure you remember what she looked like naked so you can jerk off to her later, bud."

I walked into the kitchen and told Dan the news, trying to hide my embarrassment.

"Well, at least you got to have sex, right?" he said.

I kept waiting for that to register with me, but the truth is, I felt no more like a man than I had felt before I'd had sex.

Bob came out of the office and grabbed a six-pack of Bud Lights.

"We need to have a quick chat. Grab yourself a brewski and come meet me on the upstairs balcony," he said to me before walking upstairs. "Nothing imported. I got corporate on my ass."

I grabbed a Bud Light and headed up to the balcony where Bob was sitting at an open table, with the ocean behind him. In the minute I had taken to find a beer and head upstairs, he'd already finished one beer and was halfway through another. I sat down and cracked one open.

"Nothing better on a sunny day than a beer and another dude's hard-on," he said.

"What?"

"Just messing with you. I'm not trying to pull any gay stuff on you," he said, laughing loudly. "Wait, how old are you?" he asked, his laugh immediately ceasing.

"Twenty."

He yanked the beer from my hands and set it down next to him. "Fuck me. I can't have underage drinking on the premises. You're better than that, Bob," he said to himself before chugging the rest of his open beer.

"What'd you want to talk to me about?"

"Well, I consider the kitchen staff here to be my family . . ." he started.

"What about your wife and kid?"

"Yeah, yeah. But, I mean, the kid's two. He's not even a person. And the wife's the wife. But you guys here, when one of you is cut, I bleed. And I know some girl just gave you a dick up the ass, and I know what that can do to a man. But you're on a team here, and I need to know that you are still focused and it's not going to affect your work," he said.

"Bob, I wash dishes."

"And you're one of the three best I've ever seen at it. Swear to Jesus. I'm not blowing smoke up your ass. But I'm not going to sit by and watch your skills erode because some woman has got you unfocused," he said. Then he grabbed the beer he'd confiscated from me and pounded half of it.

"I'll be focused," I said.

"Good. Because that's what a man does. He takes his shots and then he goes back into that dish pit and he scrubs the shit out of some dishes," he said, standing up and patting me on the back as he walked past me.

I went back to the kitchen, where a mountain of dishes had piled up in my absence. I put on a pair of yellow rubber gloves and turned on the hot water and got to work scrubbing. Bob was wrong: washing a lot of dishes did not make me feel like a man. Right that minute, though, neither did having sex. A rite of passage I'd expected to mean so much had left me feeling no different at all. I had no idea when I would feel like a man, or what it would take. All I could safely say was that I was a boy who had had sex, and was really, really good at washing dishes, and that would have to be enough for now.

Give the Rabbit
Its Pain Medication

After graduating from college in 2003, armed with a film degree, I moved from San Diego to Los Angeles to pursue a career in screenwriting. Unfortunately, in LA, everyone has a film degree. It's like owning a toaster, if you had to take out a loan to buy the toaster, and then when it comes time to use the toaster, it doesn't work. But I was broke and had bills to pay, so while I kept writing screenplays, hoping to break in, I took a job waiting tables at a giant, two-story Italian restaurant in Pasadena called Villa Sorriso, which was decorated with fake plants and generic pictures of Frank Sinatra. I was one of about forty waiters and bartenders, all between the ages of eighteen and thirty, save for one guy in his fifties whom I would often spot standing motionless in the center of the dining hall, lost in thought, with a look on his face that seemed to say, "Next time I need to remember to bring my gun to work so I can open fire on all these assholes."

Within a week of joining Villa Sorriso's staff, I came to the conclusion that there are basically three types of employee who work at restaurants in Los Angeles. There are people who want to be actors, people who want to be writers, and people who want to sell drugs to people who want to be actors and writers. And all three of these types usually end up having sex with each other.

I had been working at Villa Sorriso for a few months when the manager hired a new waitress: a cute brunette named Melanie who'd just moved from Colorado to pursue a career in acting. I was assigned to train her and spent a week teaching her the proper way to fold napkins, cut lemons for iced tea, and use the touch-screen computers. After we spent most of our final training day trading our favorite quotes from *The Simpsons*, I realized I had a thing for her. She was exactly the kind of girl I usually liked: smart, funny, and a little offbeat.

During a slow lunch shift the following week, I was chatting with the restaurant's bartender, Nick, an aspiring male model who looked a bit like Colin Farrell if he were made of that shiny hard plastic they use to make action figures. "Melanie's kinda hot, yeah?" I said.

"Yeah, man. She's totally cute."

"She seems cool," I said, leaning on the bar as he dried some pint glasses.

"Totally. She also sucks a mean dick."

"What?" I said, straightening up.

"Yeah, she blew me a few nights ago," he said casually.

"She's only worked here a week," I replied, my voice cracking.

"Yeah. I think it was her first day, actually. We got some drinks after work, blah blah, then she swallowed a load in my car."

"Wow."

"Oh, shit, do you have a thing for her?"

"I just thought she seemed cool," I said, slumping down on a barstool and trying to hide my disappointment.

"My bad, man. I totally would not have done that if I knew. Next chick you're into, just let me know right away and I won't hook up with her."

"No, no. That would be . . . really weird and kind of depressing. I don't really know right away, anyway. It usually takes me a little while to see if I'm into them or if they're into me, you know?"

"Yeah, but what if you just want to bone down?" he asked.

I smiled at Nick and changed the subject. The fact was, though, that I'd never had casual sex before. Oh, sure, I had always wanted to. In fact, I'd spent most of my late teens and early twenties trying to. Eventually, though, I came to the conclusion that I was the male equivalent of a Toyota Camry. You know: No one ever says, "I *have* to *have* a Toyota Camry." But most people who spend some time in a Camry start to like it. "It's pretty reliable," they think. "It doesn't have a lot of problems, and it's not bad to look at. You know what? I'd probably prefer a nicer car. But I can live with a Camry."

I had been shot down countless times after hitting on women solely because I found them attractive, and the experience was usually deflating, labor-intensive, and expensive. By the age of twenty-three I was tired of chasing women who usually chose to sleep with guys who looked like they weren't even the same species as me. At this point I generally found myself motivated to pursue a girl only after I'd decided she was relationship material and that she might also be looking for something long-term. I usually went after girls I really enjoyed talking to, who were funny and often a little shy and awkward, and so far I'd had a few girlfriends, but none had lasted more than a year.

I had my strategy, and I stuck to it—which meant I paid little attention to the cocktail waitresses at our restaurant. Their job was to get people wasted, and to do that they had to be incredibly good-looking and, more important, able to pretend that every guy, if he bought enough booze and tipped just enough, just might end up having sex with them. Because of these requirements, a lot of them seemed to be pretty unstable. Every couple weeks one of the waitresses would get fired for some minor infraction, like hurling a glass vase at a manager or snorting cocaine in the walk-in fridge. Heeding all these warning signs, I rarely spoke to the waitresses, and none of them expressed much interest in driving a Camry.

So I was shocked when, a year and a half into my tenure at Villa Sorriso, a sultry South American cocktail waitress named Simone approached me. Simone was in her early twenties, with straight jet-black hair down to the middle of her back, full lips, and bright blue eyes that gave off the kind of intense, unsettling stare I had previously seen only on Tom Cruise when he was discussing Scientology. Simone's butt protruded from the rest of her body as if it were itself a sentient being, capable of complex thought. She was so attractive that once, when I tried to pleasure myself to thoughts of her, my imagination couldn't conjure up a plausible scenario in which she would agree to have sex with me, and I was forced to stop altogether.

"Where do you live?" she said now, as I folded napkins on the bar in preparation for that night's dinner rush.

"Right outside Hollywood. Where do you live?" I asked.

"How come you never talk to me?" she said, ignoring my question.

"Um, I don't know. You guys seem really busy over there."

"You should talk to me," she said, then walked away toward two customers sitting in the lounge next to the bar.

Nick had been listening in on the exchange from behind the bar.

"That was weird," I said when he came by.

"That chick's crazy. She's trying to be a model, but she, like, also sells rabbit painkillers or something."

"What?"

"I think she has a rabbit, and the rabbit has, like, cancer or something, and she gets the painkillers for the rabbit, but then she sells them to people. I guess it gets you fucked up."

"Does she give any of them to the rabbit?" I asked.

"I don't know, man. She's smoking hot, though."

"That's a weird thing to say—'You should talk to me,' " I said, playing the conversation back in my head.

"Maybe she's into you."

"I don't think so."

I went about the rest of my shift—and then the rest of the week—without speaking to Simone. I assumed she was just another really attractive woman who wouldn't in a million years hook up with me, so I figured I'd spare myself the awkwardness that would inevitably come if I went for it.

One night the following week, while we were in the middle of a dinner rush, I was pouring a couple Diet Cokes at the soda station when I turned to find Simone standing in front of me.

"We should have dinner tonight," she said, as if we'd been talking about it for the last ten minutes.

"I'm working till close tonight," I said, as I popped lemon wedges into the sodas.

"I am too."

"So . . ."

"I don't have dinner when people say I should have dinner. I have dinner when my body tells me to have dinner," she said.

"Well, I usually have dinner at around seven, so I kinda already ate," I said.

"You can watch me eat."

"Um, well, lemme just see what time I get out of here," I said, then pushed past her with a tray filled with drinks. I knew I wasn't handling Simone's advances well, but no woman had ever come on to me so strong, and I didn't know how to respond. I didn't want to end up the laughing stock of the restaurant, but I also didn't want to pass up the chance to have sex with one of the most attractive women I'd ever met.

I dropped off the drinks, then made a beeline for Nick and told him what had happened.

"I'm telling you, I think she likes you," he said.

"Why would she like me? I haven't ever talked to her," I replied.

"Maybe that's why. Everybody tries to fuck her. I've tried to fuck her, the managers, customers. Pretty much everybody. Maybe she's just thinking, how come this guy isn't trying to fuck me? Or maybe she just likes you, man. I don't know, but you should go to dinner with her."

*　*　*

It was a busy Friday night, and I didn't get off work until one in the morning. I clocked out and took off my apron, which looked like I'd jumped on a grenade filled with Alfredo sauce. When I headed over to the cocktail waitresses' side station, Simone was at the computer, closing out a tab with a credit card.

"Hey. I'm not too beat so if you're still interested—"

"I made us a reservation at Wokano," she said, referring to a popular late-night Chinese restaurant nearby. "We're going to sit in a corner booth," she added.

"Oh. Okay. Well . . . okay."

Twenty minutes later we were sitting at a corner booth at Wokano, both of us still wearing our black work clothes. Simone looked amazing. She'd fashioned her work outfit, a black form-fitting tank top and wetsuit-tight black pants, to highlight all the appropriate areas. I was sweaty; with my silver tie loosened and my black dress shirt untucked, I looked like a used-car salesman who'd just lost ten thousand dollars gambling. She positioned herself right next to me in the booth, close enough that I could smell her perfume over the pungent odor of pesto and Parmesan cheese wafting up from stains on my shirt.

That was not the most awkward part of our dinner.

Normally, by the time I went out on a date with a girl, I'd already gotten to know her a little, and we'd hit it off enough that I'd decided it was safe to ask her out. That made it easier to hold a conversation over drinks or dinner. That night, however, Simone and I sat in silence until the waiter came to take our order.

"So, you do modeling?" I asked after he left.

"It's just a job. It's not my passion," she replied.

"What's your passion?"

"Life."

I waited for her to expand on that but was met only with silence.

"Just like . . . *living* life? Or, like . . . you want to be a life coach? I'm not really sure what you mean."

"Just everything. Every day."

Over her plate of vegetable tempura (I'd already eaten, so I stuck to a liquid second dinner), we struggled through twenty more minutes of stilted conversation. "Fish are weird," she said at one point. "Yeah," I responded, followed by a solid minute of silence. It was the highlight of the meal.

In the unlikely event that she'd been into me before dinner, I thought, there was no way she could be now. When the waiter walked by I lunged at him, shoving my credit card into his stomach before we were even presented a check. When he returned with my receipt, I quickly signed and suggested we leave.

"Can you take me to my car? I'm parked pretty far away," she said.

"Oh, sure. No problem."

We walked over to the lot where I'd parked my Ford Ranger and let her into the passenger seat. She directed me a few blocks down dark Pasadena streets until we arrived at a white Lexus. It was around two A.M., so hers was the only car still parked on the block. The streets were empty.

"Just pull up behind it," she said.

I did as I was told.

"Can you shut off the car and get out for a minute?" she asked.

"Get out?"

"Yes. I'll knock when I want you to get back in the car. Please do that. Thank you."

The first thought that ran through my head was, "I'm about to get carjacked." But my car was a pile of junk, and I was more curious about what she was doing than I was worried about losing my car. I got out and stood next to the car, rubbing my arms to keep warm.

After about a minute I heard a knock at my window, and I opened the door to get back inside. Simone was completely naked, her body gleaming under the light of the streetlamp pouring through the windshield. I felt like I was living out a bad porn narrative. And though nothing this kinky had ever happened to me before, I knew I needed to do something suave to keep us moving in the right direction.

"Whoa. You're naked," I blurted out.

In retrospect, maybe it wouldn't have mattered what I said. She leaned over from her seat, grabbed the back of my head, pulled me toward her, and started kissing me. Her lips tasted like a mixture of liquor and fried carrots. I tried to keep my eyes open as much as possible, taking as many mental snapshots as my brain could hold, as if I were seeing the Grand Canyon for the first and last time. Then I thought of something: If she was naked, I probably should be too.

As I started unbuttoning my shirt, though, she pulled away.

"I'm not going to fuck you in a car," she said.

"Oh. I totally wasn't trying to do—"

"I wanted you to see my nude body. You're very attractive to me."

"Thanks. You're very attractive to me, too," I said, instantly wanting to punch myself in the face.

"Could you get out of the car again? I don't like people seeing me change in and out of clothes."

"You're like Superman," I joked.

"Why?" she said, genuinely.

"Oh, just, you know, nobody sees Superman change."

"Why doesn't he let people see him change?" she asked.

"Well, because he tries to keep his identity secret."

"I just don't like people seeing me change in and out of clothes."

"Okay."

I got out of the car. A minute later Simone emerged, fully clothed, and gave me a really sloppy kiss on the mouth.

"We'll go out again," she said walking toward her car, my eyes trailing her. Then she got in and drove off.

I went home that night completely bewildered as to why Simone was interested in me, but confident this was my first chance at meaningless, no-strings-attached sex—and with someone I normally would have considered completely out of my league. I was so excited when I got into bed that I couldn't fall asleep for hours. If a burglar had tried to break into my house and rob me that night, I probably would have tried to high-five him and tell him about Simone as I helped carry my belongings out to his getaway car.

The next time I saw Simone was the following Friday at work. Toward the beginning of my dinner shift, as I was lighting the candles on the tables in my section, she came over and invited me back to her place when our shift was over. A few hours later, after midnight, I found my-self in her studio apartment in South Pasadena, sitting on her black leather couch, next to a large white rabbit that lay motionless on the armrest, while she poured two glasses of red wine. Still in her work outfit, she sat down next to me and made small talk for all of five minutes—most of which I spent trying to find out whether the rabbit had cancer (it did) and whether it was receiving its pain medication (unclear)—before we started making out. Ten minutes later, I was standing in her bathroom waiting for her to disrobe (still not allowed to see her change). Five minutes after that, we were on her bed hav-ing sex.

Having sex with someone is a lot like cooking a stew together; if you don't know your partner well, you just have to kind of guess what she likes and throw it in the pot, and at some point you're going to add something that's going to make the other person say, "Whoa, whoa, I don't like that." If the ingredient you toss is especially objectionable, your partner might say, "You know what? Maybe we should just stop and I'll make something for myself later." I had no idea what to throw into Simone's pot, and I hadn't exactly won Top Chef for my stew-making talents in the first place. At one point Simone stopped and said, "You should do less stuff." Then she shoved me on my back and crawled on top of me. After a couple minutes she rolled off. "Okay, now do whatever you want to me," she said, out of breath.

When we were finished, she walked into her bathroom and shut the door. I heard the shower turn on. She stayed in the bathroom for the next hour, while I sat on the bed, trying to kill time like I was in the waiting lounge of a Jiffy Lube getting my oil changed. I knew I shouldn't just go in, in case I walked in on her changing, the consequences of which I couldn't imagine but feared nonetheless.

Finally I got up and knocked on the bathroom door.

"Hey, ah, I think I'm gonna take off. I had a really nice time, though," I said.

"Me too. See you later," she yelled over the sound of a hair dryer.

After work the next Friday, we did the same thing. As we did the following Friday, and the one after that, and the one after that. I got so used to having sex on Friday nights after work that the smell of the Villa Sorriso's Friday night bacon-wrapped scallop special began to turn me on.

We never found what you might call a sexual rhythm. She mostly just wanted me to lie there and do nothing while she took advantage of the opportunity to sit on top of me. When I tried to "join the show," the results were usually horrible. This was never more evident than one time when she started yelling, "How do I get so wet? *How do I get so wet?*" Thinking she was asking me because she wanted an answer, I said, "I don't know?" Which only caused her to stop what she was doing and let out a long, deflated sigh.

I did my best to ignore things she did that made me really dislike hanging out with her, like how she never actually listened to anything I said, or how she always said "disgusting" when she walked past a homeless person. But our lack of any sort of emotional or intellectual connection eventually started to wear on me. One Friday night during the third month of our "relationship," Simone failed to show up at work. While I was disappointed not to be having sex that night, I was sort of relieved not to have to spend time with her. Toward the end of the night, after the dinner rush, I walked out the back door and into the alley to get some fresh air. The back door to the kitchen opened and the dishwasher, a young Hispanic guy named Roberto, whom everyone called "Beto," came out lugging a huge trash bag, a brown liquid dripping from its bottom.

"Hey, *guero*," he said, calling me the name all the Hispanic cooks called the white coworkers.

"Hey, Beto. How's it going?"

"Hey, *guero*, I fuck your girlfriend."

"She's not my girlfriend, but thanks for letting me know you think she's fuckable," I said, laughing.

"No. Guero, I *fuck* your girlfriend. Last month ago. I fuck her," he said, setting down the bag, then reaching his stubby arms out and thrusting his pelvis back and forth a few times in a humping motion.

"What? Really?"

"Yeah. You have the AIDS now. I am just kidding," he said, laughing.

"Wait, so, you didn't fuck her?"

"No. I fuck her. But I don't have the AIDS," he said. Then he picked up the trash bag and walked down the alley toward the Dumpster.

I felt like I should be upset. In an attempt to drudge up some feelings of anger, I even stood there trying to picture Beto on top of Simone, doing his thrusting move and laughing maniacally, in the bed where I'd planned on having sex that evening. But the most upsetting thing was, that after learning that the girl I was sleeping with was also sleeping with someone else, I discovered that I didn't care. I'd spent thousands of hours of my adolescence wishing for the scenario I'd been living for the past two months—having sex with a gorgeous woman who demanded and expected nothing more than sex from me—and yet the vacuity of our relationship was depressing me.

I considered going to her apartment to talk to her but decided it could wait a week. The next Friday I came in to work early and walked over to the cocktail waitress station hoping to find Simone, but again she wasn't there.

"Hey, Nick, is Simone here yet?" I asked.

"Uh, dude, she quit and moved to New Jersey or something," he said, as he shook a martini with one hand.

"What?"

"Yeah, I think she told the managers a couple weeks ago. She didn't say anything?"

"No. I only see her on Fridays. I just thought she was off last Friday or sick or something," I said.

"Damn. Sorry, man."

"Eh, it's okay. Just weird," I replied.

"Onto the next bone down. That's what it's all about," he said.

I was stunned. This was the second time I'd dated a waitress who'd broken up with me by skipping town altogether. I walked back to the napkin-folding station and tried to perform an autopsy on this newly deceased relationship. Normally, after a breakup, it would take me days or weeks of feeling down in the dumps, mulling over all the things that went wrong, before I started making sense of it and feeling better. But this time around, I arrived at a conclusion almost immediately: I was ready to be in a relationship that would evoke some kind of emotional response from me if I ever found out that my girlfriend had slept with a guy I worked with and/or had moved across the country without telling me. I was looking for someone I could fall in love with, someone who would give her dying rabbit painkillers.

I'd Rather Not See You Sitting Next to Me on a Friday Night

I celebrated my twenty-fifth birthday inside a tiny linen closet at the Villa Sorriso, with six other waiters and an overweight line cook named Ramon who had a teardrop tattoo on his cheek that may or may not have signaled that he killed a man in prison.

"Happy birthday," they whispered as Ramon handed me a tiramisu with a single candle flickering in the middle of it.

They were whispering because management had implemented a new rule prohibiting more than two employees from congregating on the restaurant's grounds during work hours, which made this gathering feel more like an underground Communist meeting in the 1950s than a celebration of my first quarter-century of existence. Despite the unnatural volume of our voices and the smell of cleaning supplies and dusty linens, it was a touching gesture by my friends.

"I didn't get you a present. But I shot a pig in the head on my cousin's farm and I made *carnitas*. I'll save some for you," Ramon said.

As I blew out the candle and my colleagues very quietly applauded, it dawned on me that I'd also spent my seventeenth birthday working at a restaurant, which meant I'd been working in restaurants for the last eight years. I was no longer the fresh-faced kid chasing his dreams; instead I was in danger of becoming the bitter lifer who uses dated pop-culture references and depresses younger employees. I had moved to LA to break into screenwriting, and while I'd sold a script during my first year there, these days I was doing very little writing and working seventy to eighty hours a week at the restaurant. I had upped my hours for the simple reason that I needed to save money to fix my truck, a 1999 Ford Ranger that started only half the time and had a set of brakes that made a high-pitched shrieking noise my mechanic had eloquently likened to "the sound a girl makes when you fuck her good." Coincidentally, that was a sound I'd become unfamiliar with in real life, as I'd also hit a huge dry spell with women.

I had been single so long that, on the rare occasion when I had a sex dream, it tended not to involve actual women—only visions of me pleasuring myself to pornography, as if my brain had forgotten what sex was. I was so desperate to be in a relationship that, when I did go out on dates, I usually scared off my companions by trying to lock them down for future dates right away, or asking them repeatedly, "Are you having fun?" There's nothing less fun than someone asking if you're having it.

My life had fallen into a rut so slowly that I didn't even know it was happening, until I walked out of that linen closet to go take the orders of a dining room full of hungry septuagenarians and realized I was anywhere but where I wanted to be.

A few weeks after my birthday, I found myself with the first weekend I'd had off in months. All my friends were working at the restaurant and there was no way I was going to spend that free time alone in my dumpy ground-floor apartment in Hollywood—which had begun to stink more than usual, thanks to my pothead neighbor's new favorite hobby, which was catching rats with a mousetrap, then hurling their corpses over the fence into my backyard when he thought I wasn't looking. When I caught him in the act, he pretended to be offended. "Maybe it jumped, and thought there was gonna be water on the other side, but then there wasn't and it died or something?" So, with nowhere to go and in need of a break from LA, I tossed some clothes into a trash bag and headed down to my parents' house in San Diego.

I pulled up to their house midday on Friday and knocked on the front door. My dad opened it and stood in front of me wearing a gray sweatsuit with royal-blue racer stripes.

"Whoa. What in the fuck are you doing here?" he said.

"Just thought I'd come down and see you guys for a couple days. Sort of spur of the moment," I replied.

"Oh. Well, all right. Good to see you, son. Come on in and quiet yourself. I'm watching a show about dark matter."

After I set my things down I called my best friends Dan and Ryan, who still lived in San Diego, to see what they were up to. Unfortunately Dan was going out of town with his girlfriend to visit her parents, and Ryan was trying to track down a man with a goat so that he could talk the guy into letting him milk it. He asked if I wanted to join him, but it seemed like there were a lot of ways for that to end badly, so I declined.

My mom came home from work a couple hours later and was thrilled to see me. She whipped up some pesto and the three of us took our seats around the dinner table in the living room.

"It's such a nice surprise to see you, Justy. What are you doing down here?" my mom asked, dumping a ladle full of pasta onto my plate.

"He hates LA," my dad said.

"I don't hate LA," I replied.

"Look, I'm on your side. All that traffic, people pissing and shitting on the street. No kind of place to live," he said.

"No one is going to the bathroom on the street, Sam," my mom said.

"Bullshit. There's rivers of excrement. I could fucking raft down them. Trust me. I know. Connie and I had an apartment in Brentwood for three years," he said, referring to his first wife.

My dad didn't talk about Connie very often. She had died of cancer when my brothers were one and three years old. Connie's death, and the seven years that followed before my dad met my mother, was a part of his life he didn't revisit often, and one I knew almost nothing about. On the rare occasion when he mentioned Connie, I tried as gently as I could to ask about his life with her.

"Did Connie live in this house?"

"I bought it for her. Then she passed and it was just me and your brothers. They were in diapers," he said.

"You should have seen this place when we started dating," my mom chimed in. "Every room was just medical books and fishing poles, and the only thing in the cupboards was peanut butter," she added, with a big smile on her face.

"Guess what? I like medical books, fishing, and fucking peanut butter. And plus, I didn't give a shit. I had given up on women," he added.

"Oh, please. You drove an Alfa Romeo Spider convertible and wore a leather jacket," my mom said.

"I said I gave up on women, not on getting laid," he replied.

"You wore a leather jacket?" I said, laughing.

"Yeah, it's a garment commonly worn by individuals who get laid."

"You'd be surprised. He's very charming," my mom said, getting up to retrieve something from the kitchen, leaving me and my dad alone.

"How long after Connie died did you start dating?" I asked.

"A while. Not sure exactly, but a while."

"Did you go out a lot?"

"Oh, yeah. I went up and down this goddamn city. I was going out a couple times a week at least."

"What'd you do about Dan and Evan?" I asked.

"I took them with me and had my dates wipe their shitty asses. What do you think? I put them to bed, then hired a babysitter."

"Were any of them girlfriends, or just a few dates and that was it?" I asked.

"Mostly that," he said, taking a drink from his bourbon.

"Why do you think none of them worked out?"

"Son, my wife was dead and I was lonely. That's a pretty shitty place to start from," he said.

I had never before heard my father confess to being lonely. This is a man who wakes up at 4:30 in the morning for the sole purpose of spending a few extra minutes alone. He even takes vacations alone. "It doesn't matter where I go, just as long as no one goes with me," he says. "I could vacation in my own home if everyone would leave me the fuck alone." I also couldn't imagine him dating. He hates small talk, which is exactly what most people suffer through on first dates. I wanted to know how he'd gone from a guy lonely enough to engage in a conversation he hated, with a woman he probably didn't care about, to a guy comfortable enough with himself to walk into restaurants and ask for a "table for one . . . with no other chairs."

With little else to do, I spent the next two days thinking about my dad's transformation while going to the beach and taking hikes with my family's dog, Angus. On Sunday night, after a restful, rejuvenating couple days, I dumped my freshly laundered clothes into a new trash bag, threw it in the passenger seat of my truck, and said good-bye to my parents on the front porch. When I went to give my dad a hug, he handed me a check. It was for seven hundred dollars, and on the memo line he had written, "to fix your fucking car."

"Oh, wow, no, you don't have to do that. I've been saving up," I said.

"Let's not go through the fucking dog and pony show here. You're broke, I got a little money, your car is a piece of shit that needs to be fixed. Is any of that incorrect?" he asked.

"No," I said.

"Okay then."

"Thank you."

"You're welcome. I know you been working like crazy, so let me suggest something."

"Sure."

"Fix your car, cut back on some of your hours, and take a little time for yourself. Get your shit right. I like seeing you, but I'd rather not on a Friday night. Catch my drift?" he asked.

"Yeah," I replied.

"You are welcome here any time," my mom interjected.

"Well, of course he is. That's not what I was saying," he said.

"I know that, but I wanted to make sure he knew that," she replied.

"He knew it. He's not slow. Tell her you get fucking subtext," he said to me.

"I understand subtext, Mom."

"There you go. Now get the hell out of here. I'm taking your mom out to dinner," he said.

The next day, back in LA, I took my car to the shop. They spent a week fixing everything from the starter to the air-conditioning, which for years had been blowing warm, uriney air at my face. I cut my shifts at the restaurant back to five nights a week and suddenly found myself with more energy and two full days off on my hands.

As soon as I had a moment to myself, I started thinking about what I was doing in LA. I called myself a writer, but so did my rat-hurling neighbor. In fact, when I'd run into him in the parking garage a few weeks before, he'd told me he was almost finished writing a comic screenplay about "an alien that comes to earth but people just think he's a gay." If this guy could finish *Gaylien* (his title, not mine), I told myself, I had to be able to finish the scripts I'd been working on. I was determined not to spend any more birthdays inside a closet, eating the same preservative-laden dessert that my restaurant gave away for free to children under five who ordered the chicken fingers. I decided to pour myself into my writing.

Over the next eight months, I spent any free time I had either working on a screenplay or trying to figure out if I was going to go bald. Both endeavors proved productive: I finished one script and concluded that my head hair would soon be a thing of the past. My dry spell with women continued, but I did my best not to obsess over it. I did develop a recurring dream in which a woman in a tree hurled oranges at me while repeatedly screaming, "I hate you, Jason!" Although that's not my name, I was fairly confident that my penis was sending me a message that it was furious at me for rendering it useless.

Nevertheless, with each passing day, I had an easier time focusing on writing and having fun doing it. By the end of those eight months, I went to bed at night excited to wake up the next day and start writing again. I'm not sure if this is what my dad had meant when he told me to "get my shit right," but at least I was no longer feeling the urge to toss my clothes in a trash bag and head to my parents' house in San Diego on a Friday night.

A few weeks after that, an artist friend of mine named Theresa invited me to a show of her work at a gallery on Wilshire Boulevard in LA.

The gallery was inside a refurbished warehouse and held a good-sized crowd, of which I was probably the only guy who didn't have a mustache, a twenty-four-inch waist, and either a scarf or a porkpie hat. I felt like I'd walked into a Wes Anderson movie. So, after saying hello to Theresa and looking at her work, I was ready to take off. But then, just before I left, I noticed a friend of Theresa's standing by herself in the middle of the show, looking as lost as I felt.

Her name was Amanda. I'd met her once before when she had come to visit Theresa from San Francisco for a couple days, but had spoken to her only briefly. She had wavy brown hair that fell just past her shoulders and a cherubic face that was lit up by two sparkly light-blue-green eyes. Unlike the rest of the girls in the party, she had actual curves that filled out the navy-blue dress she was wearing. She flashed a nervous smile at me and gave one of those quick waves you give someone when you're not sure if he remembers you. I smiled and waved back, and she walked over to where I was standing, near the exit.

"I don't know anyone here, and everyone is cooler than me," she said.

"So you picked the least cool guy in the place to come talk to," I replied.

"We can be uncool together," she said.

I stayed at the show for another hour talking to Amanda. She was quick and funny and a little self-deprecating, but not in a way that seemed like a defense mechanism for a truckload of self-loathing. I tried my best not to weird her out and largely succeeded, except perhaps for one point when I described myself as looking like "Jason

Biggs with a terminal illness." It was the first time in as long as I could remember that I'd enjoyed a relaxed conversation with a woman.

"We should hang out sometime," I said as I was leaving.

"I'm flying back to San Francisco tomorrow," she replied.

"Maybe someone will call in a bomb threat and you'll have to stay another night. Wow. That was a really terrible joke. I don't know why I said that."

"No, bomb jokes are always funny to people who are about to board a plane," she said, laughing. "I wouldn't worry, anyway. You've told way worse jokes within this last hour." She gave me a hug good-bye.

I thought about Amanda quite a bit over the next few days. The situation seemed kind of hopeless, since she lived five hundred miles away, but my brain didn't want to acknowledge the distance. I tried to put her out of my mind, to buckle down and finish a second screenplay I was working on. Then, a couple days later, as I was working in my living room, I heard a loud clang on my barbecue. I walked out to my backyard to find a rat splattered on the top of my grill.

"Hey! Stop throwing rats in my yard!" I yelled over the fence.

There was no answer so I grabbed an old newspaper from the recycling bin, used it to pick up the rat corpse, and tossed it back over the fence.

"Whoa, whoa, whoa!" I heard my neighbor yell from behind the fence.

"Dude! Stop it! I've had enough of this crap!" I shouted.

"Okay. Shit. Chill out, man. I'm sorry. You don't need to Nolan Ryan that shit at me, man."

I went inside, washed my hands, and felt a huge sense of accomplishment. Sure, maybe getting a man to stop throwing dead rats into my yard wasn't exactly on par with building schools for underprivileged Iraqi children, but at the time it felt significant and invigorating. I sat back down at my computer, opened up my Gmail, and sent Amanda an e-mail with the subject line, "I just threw a dead rat at my neighbor."

Don't Make Me Take Up Residence in Your Fantasy Land

When I was thirteen, my dad barged into my room after dinner one night while I was doing homework. Before I could set my pencil down, he said: "You've been jerking off a lot."

"What? What are you talking about?" I shrieked.

"Relax. I could give a shit. Good for you that you can find the time. I can't get a second to myself. But there's two things I need you to know: one, I'm going to be doing the laundry for the next few months because your mom's studying for the bar exam; and two, I'll be god-damned if I'm gonna reach down into the laundry basket and pick up a towel that's crunchy like a fucking Dorito 'cause you did your business in it, okay?"

He stared down at me. I was frozen in shock and humiliation.

"Say okay. I need to hear verbal confirmation," he said.

"Okay," my voice cracked.

"Thank you. Now that we got that unfortunate business out of the way, I figured now'd be a halfway decent time to bring up something else," he continued.

"Really, I don't do that, though," I interjected.

"Are we going to talk like men or do I have to take up residence in your fantasy land?"

"What were you going to say, Dad?"

"Clearly your hormones are bouncing around like a puppy with two dicks. But I'm not here to give you some bullshit talk about women. There are three billion of them, and to generalize that many people with some blanket statement is the definition of being an asshole. Women are all different, so I don't have any advice on them. But I feel fairly qualified to give you some advice about yourself."

"Okay," I sighed.

"Oh, I'm sorry, am I keeping you from a fucking appointment with the head of marketing or something?"

I sat back in my chair and put my feet up on the bed to signify my surrender.

"Someday you're going to meet a fine woman. And hopefully, if I haven't completely fucked you up, you're going to recognize that. But I have never seen a human being drive himself more batshit than you when it's time to make a decision. Every time you order lunch it's like you're presiding over the fucking Cuban missile crisis."

"I'm a picky eater," I said.

"You're a picky everything. Probably my fault. Did my best. Not gonna dwell on it, though. Which brings me to my point. Someday you're gonna go stupid for a woman. And when you do, do me this one favor: don't get all caught up in the bullshit that's going on in your head. If it's right, then you put on your fuckin' big-boy pants and you go for it."

Twelve years later, I felt, for the first time in my life, like my dad's prediction had come true: I was going stupid for a woman. Before meeting Amanda, I'd done plenty of stupid things *for* women, like the time I lent my car to my first girlfriend's little brother, who used it to mule a thousand dollars of Viagra he bought in Tijuana back across the border. But even when I was infatuated with a girl in the past, she never became the only thing I could think about. With Amanda, everything changed.

In the month since I'd run into her at the gallery show, she and I had exchanged e-mails every day. We e-mailed about everything from past relationships to major league baseball to what scenario would make it okay to eat your family dog. (I said the apocalypse; she argued that I'd never survive the apocalypse because of my allergies, so why eat my only companion just so I could live a few more dark days?) I became so enamored of our discourse that I would sit down at my wobbly forty-dollar Ikea desk in the corner of my bedroom and spend two hours drafting, rewriting, and polishing a five-thousand-word e-mail—only to wake up the next day and find one just as long from her. I couldn't stop thinking about her. I thought about what she might be doing, what she was thinking, where she was *right then*. I thought about what it would be like to date her, or even be married to her. I had gone stupid. And we were just getting to know each other.

I lay in bed one night, a month into our e-relationship, driving myself crazy wondering if she'd ever consider moving to Los Angeles and how it would work if she didn't. I realized I needed to stop. My obsession was unhealthy; and I was setting myself up for potential heartbreak. I needed to think critically. I took a deep breath, tried to clear my head of all my hopes and fears, and focused on the most logical question I could ask myself: How could I possibly like her as much as I felt I did? The answer I came up with was that there was no way I could. In twenty seconds I went from head over heels to completely cold feet.

I didn't e-mail her the next day. It was the first day I had missed in a month. If I backed off and put a little distance between us, I figured, maybe I could control myself, get a better handle on the situation. Plus, I wasn't even sure how Amanda felt about me, and I was already hoping our kids would get her nose instead of mine. But I never got the chance to take a breather. The very next day, Amanda sent me this note: "I would love it if you would come see me in San Francisco this weekend. I'm having a Halloween party. I'm going to be dressed as Fergie from the Black Eyed Peas after she peed her pants on stage. Just in case you were thinking of going as that."

Flights from LA to San Francisco started at a hundred bucks. I currently had one hundred and thirty-three dollars in my bank account. I knew that because I checked it online every day leading up to the end of the month. I lived in constant fear of my bank balance.

I always got a paycheck around the first of the month, which usually gave me just enough money to pay my rent if I didn't miss any shifts, but going to visit Amanda would definitely make me miss at least one. Still, I couldn't shake how much I wanted to see her.

I decided to look online to see if I could find a sale on flights. I couldn't. The cheapest was a hundred and fifty bucks, which would put me seventeen dollars in the red. But way down on the Google search results page was an ad for a company called Megabus, which was offering one-dollar round-trip rides from L.A. to San Francisco for the first ten people who bought tickets. There was one left for the upcoming weekend. I bought it and e-mailed Amanda to let her know I was coming.

That Saturday morning I stuffed a weekend's worth of clothes in a backpack and headed over to Union Station in downtown Los Angeles, where I came upon a large blue bus emblazoned with a giant pig wearing a bus driver's costume. I showed my ticket to the driver, who grunted and motioned for me to take a seat. The bus was dark and cold, yet somehow humid, like the dank pit where Buffalo Bill keeps his victims in *The Silence of the Lambs*. The forty or so seats were mostly empty, save for about ten occupied by fellow travelers, all of whom looked like they were fleeing LA rather than visiting San Francisco.

As I walked down the center aisle to find a seat, a man with a sleeveless T-shirt and one eye swollen shut looked at me, then put his feet up on the seat next to him. I headed all the way to the back, three rows away from the nearest passenger, sat down, and cracked open a book. Then, just before we were about to head out, a man in a wool cap carrying only a single fishing pole got on the bus, walked all the way to the back, and sat down right next to me. I thought about getting up to move, but then worried I'd insult him, and he didn't look like the type of guy who took insults well.

For the next eight hours we sat in silence next to each other, save for a ten-minute break when we stopped off at a roadside Burger King. He stared straight ahead, motionless the entire time, with his hands in his pockets. I had planned to sleep, but I kept hearing the noise of something he was fidgeting with in his pants and started worrying that I wouldn't be able to protect myself if it turned out to be some kind of weapon and he was in a stabbing mood, which didn't look implausible.

Finally, at around five P.M., San Francisco's Transamerica Pyramid and surrounding skyline appeared on the horizon. The fisherman shifted his weight and turned to me for the first time.

"Why are you here?" he said in a guttural voice.

"Like, why am I going to San Francisco? Or why am I on this bus?" I asked, sliding away from him and preparing for a defensive maneuver.

"San Francisco."

"I'm visiting someone."

"Do you enjoy this bus?" he asked.

"Do I enjoy it? I mean, not really. Do you?"

"I paid one dollar. For one dollar I would let them rape me on this bus," he said, then broke into an uncomfortably boisterous laugh, as if he were in the audience of an episode of *Cheers*.

Amanda had given me directions from the bus station to her house via subway, and after getting on the wrong train twice in a row, I groggily walked up to an old Victorian apartment building near the Castro district. Door-to-door, it had taken me eleven hours to get to her. I was in a horrible mood, and I looked and smelled like a nineteenth-century miner who'd just traveled to San Francisco by boat to mine for gold. My head was throbbing as I walked up the stairs to her second floor apartment and knocked on the door.

The door flung open. Amanda grabbed me with both arms and squeezed.

"You're here!" she said, holding on to me in the doorway. "How was the trip?"

"It was long," I replied.

She grabbed my bags from me and led me into her apartment.

"Ugh. That sucks. Well, I'm really excited you're here. I'm gonna put your stuff in my room. We have to grab some booze for the party, and I figured we could stop at a thrift store, too, so you could buy some stuff for a costume. Did you think of any ideas on the way up?"

"No. I sat next to a rapist."

"What?"

"He might not have been a rapist. I shouldn't say that. He just seemed like it. Anyway, I didn't think about a costume."

"Oh. Well, okay."

Amanda set my bags down in a small, plaster-walled room, which looked like a converted dining area, now occupied by a neatly made bed that smelled like the opposite of me. I walked back down the hall to the lone bathroom. As I washed my hands and ran water over my face, I started thinking about having to make that bus trip several times a month. And then about how broke I was. And then it hit me that, last time I'd checked my bank account, I'd forgotten to account for my phone bill, which I had on auto-pay. I asked Amanda if I could jump on her computer, and when I did my online balance confirmed my anxiety. I now had fifty-four dollars in my account to last me for the rest of the month, and I still needed a Halloween costume.

I also realized I hadn't really been putting on a good showing for Amanda. I had to buck up—especially because her costume was perfect, right down to the shape of the urine stain on the crotch, which perfectly mirrored the one in the photo of the soiled rock star she'd clipped out of a celebrity magazine. I should have been excited to be there with Amanda, after all those weeks of thinking of little else, but I was so consumed with worrying about money that all I could think about was that I'd never be able to afford the travel and the missed work it would take to date her, even if I was willing to take the dollar bus filled with suspected criminals. Determined to create the cheapest costume possible, when we got to the thrift store I ended up buying a three-dollar pair of brown slacks, a two-dollar shirt, and a thirty-cent hand broom. Then I scooped some black grease from the inside of a tire on the sidewalk in front of her house, rubbed it on my face, and called myself a chimney sweep. An hour later her tiny apartment filled with thirty or forty costumed partygoers.

For the next couple of hours, I stood silently next to Amanda as she made her rounds, seeing all of her friends. I felt like it was my first day on the job and I was shadowing my trainer. The place was jammed; '90s rap music was blasting out of the small living room, where a tightly packed dance party had broken out. Despite the noise and crowd, Amanda was doing her best to introduce me to her friends and make sure I had a good time. And, like a total self-consumed jerk, I was no help whatsoever.

"People are liking your costume," Amanda said as she poured vodka into two plastic red Solo cups.

"Really? Who told you that?" I replied.

"You know, just people at the party."

"Nobody told you they liked my costume, did they?"

"No. But it was a vibe I got."

Meeting your date's friends for the first time is like playing poker; you have to read each one of them, and then put forth just the right amount of conversation. If you go all in on someone who just wanted to say hi, you'll risk seeming pushy and desperate. If you fold and stand there silent when you're introduced to her chatty best friend, you might come off as weird and antisocial. And if you put on a face that says "Don't come near me," everyone else will fold—which is what was happening to me. I was tired and nervous, it was loud, and I was talking myself out of every fantasy that had consumed me through those past couple weeks. I was failing miserably, and Amanda could see it.

After a while, she grabbed my arm and pulled me toward the dance floor. But just as she did, I felt the Burger King Chicken Griller I'd eaten during the one middle-of-nowhere stop on the bus ride suddenly snap awake in my stomach. It wanted out, and it wanted out now. Unfortunately, it didn't seem to be headed out the way it came in. At least if I puked, I could blame it on alcohol or bad food. It happens: people puke all the time at parties. No one gets explosive diarrhea.

Amanda tried to pull me toward her, but I didn't move.

"Let's dance," she yelled over the music.

"I, uh—I think I need to use your bathroom," I said.

"You know where it is, right?"

"Yeah. I'll be right back."

I quickly walked down the hall. With every step, my need to avail myself of her toilet grew exponentially, the way earthquakes get ten times more devastating with every tenth of a point on the Richter scale. I opened the bathroom door, only to find a man dressed as Gandalf from *Lord of the Rings* with his back to me, peeing. I quickly closed the door and hurried back to Amanda, who was on the dance floor with a few friends, moving to the thumping bass of Digital Underground's "Humpty Dance." I pulled her aside.

"Does your bathroom have a lock on the door?" I yelled.

"No. But just close it. No one's gonna come in, I promise."

"So there's no way to lock it?" I said, starting to panic.

"Well, no. Why, what's wrong?"

"I just . . . I'm not feeling well and I sort of need to spend a little while in there, and I really can't have somebody coming in. Is there like a chair or something I can borrow to keep it closed?"

"A chair? You want to barricade the door closed?"

"I just don't want anyone to come in."

"I don't think anyone's going to come in, but I guess if you're worried I could stand next to the door and guard it," she said.

"Is that weird?" I asked.

"Yes. That's really weird."

"I'm really sorry, but can you do that?"

She nodded and I immediately turned, swam through a group of a half dozen girls dressed as a six-pack of Budweiser—planting my palms on their backs and shoving off them like I was climbing up a rocky hillside—and hustled toward the bathroom with Amanda close behind. I reached the door and turned to find her right behind me.

"Good luck. We're all pulling for you," she said, holding back a laugh.

I feigned a smile, but I had no time to waste. I burst into the bathroom and onto the toilet. And that is where I sat for the next ten minutes as my body expressed its distaste for rest-stop Burger King. In no uncertain terms.

As I sat there relieving myself, I started mulling over everything that had led me to this point. I was broke. I hated traveling. I barely knew Amanda. And yet for some reason I'd allowed myself to blow our relationship out of proportion in my mind and convinced myself that I could make things work with her. Even by coming to see her, I was leading her on. To be fair to her, I had to end this.

Just as I finished and was pulling up my pants, I heard the door handle jiggle.

"No, no! There's somebody in there," I heard Amanda's muffled voice insist.

"So you're next in line?" another voice asked her.

"Uh—yeah."

She didn't need to go to the bathroom. She probably decided it would be much more humiliating to say, "No, I'm guarding the door for this guy I'm dating while he poops." But now she would have to come in after me—which would be much, much worse than a stranger walking in during my session.

I quickly washed my hands, grabbed a pack of matches, and lit three of them in quick, desperate succession. I pried open the only window as far open as it would go with the force of someone trying to rip it from its hinges. Then I opened the bathroom door, where Amanda—and three others—were waiting.

As she walked in, I gave her a look that said, "I am so, so sorry." Then I waited outside the bathroom. A minute later came a flush; then Amanda reappeared, with the stunned look of a rookie cop leaving the scene of her first homicide.

To make matters worse, as the next guy in line stepped into the bathroom, he let out a resounding "Whoa!" The two other people waiting looked accusingly at Amanda.

We walked down the hall and back into the party.

"Do you want to go outside for a second?" I shouted over the music.

We went out onto a small balcony, overlooking a courtyard thirty feet below that was littered with cigarette butts.

"You owe me. Like, a lot. There are now people walking around thinking I took, no offense, a really, really nasty poo in the middle of a party I was throwing. That is some above-and-beyond stuff I did right there," she said.

"I am really sorry. I can go tell them it was me."

"Yeah, that sounds like that would make things less weird," she said, laughing.

"Again, I can't tell you how sorry I am. What can I do to make it up to you?"

"How about you just loosen up a little bit and we have a good time?"

That didn't really seem possible, and although this didn't seem like the best time to bring up my fear that a relationship between us could never work, it seemed worse to pretend everything was fine. I had never been very good at doing that anyway.

"I kinda wanted to talk to you about that," I said.

"About what?" she asked.

"I know I've been a little weird since I got up here, and I mean, I've been thinking about how you live in San Francisco and I live in LA, and we're both broke, and clearly I don't travel well, as you just witnessed, and I don't know . . ."

I trailed off in a cowardly fashion, hoping she would finish the thought for me.

"So then it won't work," she said matter-of-factly.

"Well, that's what I'm saying I'm worried about."

"Right, but either it won't work, or it will. I don't know you super well, but what I know I really like, and that's why I wanted you to come up here. Do you feel the same way about me, or no?"

Not once in the past few hours had I asked myself that question. In fact, I had basically asked myself every other question I could think of. I had focused on all the reasons why our relationship would be tough. But I'd avoided the one thing that had brought me here in the first place. Hearing her ask me point-blank how I felt about her shoved all my anxieties out of the way. The answer to her question popped into my head as if it had sprung from a cage.

"Yeah, I do. I really like you, too. That's why I wanted to come up here."

"All right. Well, why don't we keep coming to see each other until we don't like doing it, and if that other stuff is just too hard to get past, then I guess we'll deal with it then. We're not making any big decisions."

"I'm down with that. Sorry, I kinda freaked out. I'm pretty neurotic," I said.

"Yeah, I picked up on that when you asked me to guard the door while you pooped," she said.

I leaned in to kiss her and she backed away.

"No, no. I taste like booze and Thai food. Super gross. We'll make out later," she said, and we walked back inside and onto the dance floor.

For the first time that night I felt unencumbered. I was simply happy to be around Amanda and even happier that she wanted to be around me. The beginning of House of Pain's "Jump Around" began to play and Amanda grabbed me.

"It's like a law that white people have to dance to this. FYI, I told people we're dating," she said, as she pulled me close to her.

Four years later, I sat down across from my father at a restaurant on the San Diego Harbor and told him I was going to put on my big-boy pants and propose to the first and only woman I'd gone stupid for.

Do You Know
What Makes a
Shitty Scientist?

In the four years since Amanda and I first got together at her Halloween party in San Francisco, we'd been through bus rides; plane flights; one breakup; one makeup; a Christmas at my parents' house where my dad told her a twenty-minute story about the "most diseased penis" he'd seen in forty-eight years of medicine; a Thanksgiving at her parents' house where I told the story of my dad telling *her* that story, which proved to be just as inappropriate; two thousand-plus hours watching HGTV; a couple of funerals; way too many weddings; and at least three more dire occasions when she had to guard a bathroom entrance for me.

Now we were living together in a small apartment in a sleepy neighborhood of San Diego called North Park. She was in a PhD program in San Diego, and I was between jobs writing for bad television shows. When you move in with someone, you can't hide all the weird and annoying things you do, and while sometimes that unveiling ruins the relationship, often it seals the deal. It's like being a meat eater and having your vegetarian friend e-mail you one of those videos that shows you what goes on behind the scenes at a slaughterhouse; if you can make it past that, you'll probably be a meat eater for life.

Amanda and I found that we were a great team. When I would get too neurotic, her blunt, confident, unflinching loyalty would smack me back to sanity, like when she'd tell me, "Just do what you think is right, and I'll always have your back. Unless what you think is right is some other girl. 'Cause then I'll stab both of you and go to jail." When she would get stressed out because she put so much pressure on herself to succeed, I'd be there to make her laugh and tell her, "I'll still love you if you're a failure. Just not as much."

After a few months living together we started to talk about marriage, and as soon as we did, I realized that marrying Amanda was something I wanted to do, not just the next logical move. I confidently conceived of a plan for how I would propose, and I bought a ring. When I finally held the ring in my hand, though, I was struck by the magnitude of what I was about to do, and my anxiety wormed its way back into the equation. When I invited my dad to lunch at Pizza Nova, I hadn't yet told anyone else about my plans; I was looking for affirmation from the only person I could count on to give me a straight answer. And after our lunch I took my dad's advice and spent the afternoon in Balboa Park looking back over all my experiences with love, sex, and yearning, in hopes of gaining confidence in my decision.

What jumped out at me, as I looked back, was that I'd spent most of my time in relationships trying not to screw them up. I was like a backup quarterback, just happy to be sitting there holding the clipboard and wearing a headset, but much too scared to get in the game and play. And as I sat there in that park I realized just how much that had sucked. For years, I'd been so busy worrying about whether I might do or say something stupid—like drawing a picture of a dog crapping on a girl's head—that I never had any fun.

With Amanda, I was finally having fun. And it wasn't as if I'd consciously decided to stop worrying. She put me at ease, and my desire to enjoy my time with her superseded all the fears that usually rattled around in my head. She was the only person I'd ever met who made me feel calm and confident, like one of the guys in the *Ocean's Eleven* movies (and not just the little curly-haired guy who's there because he's good with numbers). And as I headed out of the park six hours later, as the sun was setting, I knew I wanted to marry Amanda. I also knew I'd better go before the security guard in the park decided this guy roaming the park aimlessly was some kind of schizophrenic or pedophile.

Amanda was visiting San Francisco that weekend, and I'd arranged to surprise her on Sunday at a brunch spot in the Mission district called Foreign Cinema, where I would pop the question. In order to make my 10:30 A.M. reservation in San Francisco, I had booked a seven o'clock flight from San Diego, which meant I had to wake up at five. That night, I plugged in my cell phone to charge it, then set two alarms on it, one for 5:00 and one for 5:10, just in case I slept through the first one. Then I hit the sack.

When I woke up in the middle of the night to use the bathroom, I discovered that the power had gone out. I scrambled around in the dark and grabbed my cell. It was shortly after 1 A.M. and my phone only had one bar of battery left. I had to go someplace where I could charge my phone and be sure my alarm would wake me up. I got out of bed, grabbed the ring box off my dresser, threw on the dress pants and pale blue button-down shirt I'd laid out the night before, and headed out the door.

Twenty minutes later, I pulled into my parents' driveway. I walked up the narrow path to their front door as quietly as I could, slid my key into the lock, and gingerly opened the door. It was pitch-black inside. I made an immediate right into the living room with my hands in front of me to avoid bumping into anything.

"You better be fucking related to me," I heard my dad say from somewhere in the room.

"It's me! It's Justin!" I said, my heart leaping into my throat.

Suddenly a lamp went on. My dad was sitting in his recliner, wearing his casual sweats (gray, no action stripes), holding a mug filled with a steaming hot toddy I could smell across the room.

"Sorry. I didn't know anybody was awake," I said.

"Do you realize I'm a crazy son of a bitch who owns a shotgun and hates shadowy figures walking around in his fucking home?"

"I'm sorry. I figured everyone was sleeping. I was trying not to wake anybody up."

"Well, what the hell are you doing here, son?"

I explained to him about the power going out, and needing to charge my cell phone so my alarm would go off so I'd wake up in time for the flight to San Francisco so I could get to the Mission and—

"All right, all right, I don't need you to perform a fucking monologue," he said. "Crash on the couch, charge your phone, set your alarm, and I'll make sure you're up in time and give you a lift to the airport." He took a final sip of his hot toddy and sauntered down the hallway to his bedroom. I plugged my phone into the nearest outlet, removed my pants and shirt so as not to wrinkle them, lay down on the couch, shut my eyes, and fell asleep.

I awoke to my father standing above me in the same clothes, drinking a mug that was now filled with coffee, holding a thick book in his hand.

"It's go time," he said, poking me in the face with the book.

"Did I sleep through my alarm?" I said, still not totally awake.

"No idea."

"What time is it?" I asked, rubbing my eyes.

"Four A.M."

"Dad, I set my alarm for five thirty. I'm really tired," I replied, closing my eyes and turning away from him.

"Bullshit. It's all in your head. In med school I used to sleep an hour a night and get up the next day to deliver a fucking child."

"That sounds very irresponsible," I said, pulling my T-shirt over my head in hopes he'd leave me alone.

"Get up. I made breakfast," he said, flipping on a switch that caused the light to blast through my eyelids.

There was no chance I was going to be allowed to get back to sleep, so I sat up and groggily made my way over to the breakfast table, where there were two plates, each filled with at least ten pieces of bacon and one piece of toasted multigrain bread. My dad handed me a mug of steaming coffee. Then he sat down across from me and opened up the book he had poked me with, a large biography of Harry Truman. He sat silently reading as he periodically brought a slice of bacon to his lips. After about a minute, I couldn't stand it anymore.

"You woke me up to eat breakfast and you don't want to talk or anything? You just want to . . . eat here in silence?" I asked.

"Sounds like a plan," he said, not taking his eyes away from the book.

"Well," I continued. "I took your advice and spent all day in the park thinking about proposing."

"Must have gone well, since you're going through with it," he mumbled, as he flipped a page and continued reading.

"It did. I feel like I'm one hundred percent sure. She's it. That's it."

His head jerked up from his book and he stared at me, his eyebrows creasing together to form what looked like a caterpillar crawling across his forehead.

"That is a load of horseshit," he said, closing his book and setting it on the table.

"What? No, it's not."

"You're a hundred percent sure this marriage will work out?" he asked.

"What kind of question is that?"

"You know what makes a shitty scientist?"

"No. I don't know. I don't care. I don't want to have this conversation right now," I snapped.

"Kindly calm the fuck down and eat your bacon."

I pushed my plate in front of me an inch, sat back in my chair, and defiantly crossed my arms, as if refusing to eat any more bacon would register my displeasure.

"A shitty scientist goes into an experiment determined to get a specific result."

"Don't all scientists do that? Isn't that what a hypothesis is?" I responded.

"What? No. What the fuck? Jesus Christ. Fucking public schools. A hypothesis is when the scientist says, 'This is what I think *might* happen.' "

"Right."

"But when you go into an experiment and you're abso-fucking-lutely sure you're going to be right, the experiment inevitably goes to shit, because you're not prepared for anything unexpected. Then, when something fucked-up does happen—and it will—you either don't see it, or you just pretend like it never happened because you refuse to believe you could have fucked up. And you know what that does?" he asked.

"Ruins your experiment?"

"Bingo. So the only way to run an experiment successfully is to start by accepting the fact that your experiment might fail."

I sat quietly, digesting what I'd just heard.

"I'm sayin' marriage is the same thing," he said.

"Yeah, I gathered that."

"Well, shit, you didn't know what the fuck a hypothesis was. Just trying to make sure you grasp the analogy."

"So how do you make sure it doesn't fail?" I asked.

"Beats the dog shit out of me. I mostly just try to remember that I found someone who seems to enjoy all the bullshit that comes with being married to me, so I should probably be real fucking nice. Also I don't go in the bathroom and shit when she's taking a shower."

"I feel good about proposing," I said.

"Good, you should. She's a fine woman," he said.

"I really hate it when you say that. It sounds like you're talking about a horse."

He laughed. "Go shower so you don't smell like hell when you propose to your wife." Then he grabbed his Harry Truman book and resumed reading.

An hour and a half later, my dad pulled his Chevy Blazer up to the loading zone in front of San Diego International Airport. It was still dark outside.

"Thanks for the ride," I said as I stepped out of the car.

"Not a problem. Last thing I'll say: Try not to be too sweaty when you ask. It's disconcerting—it's an evolutionary sign of weakness. Hits her on the subconscious level."

"Um, okay."

I shut the passenger door and he drove off.

I entered the airport and breezed through check-in since I had no carry-on luggage. When I got to security, I put only two things in the plastic bin for scanning: my cell phone and the little black box containing my ring. The portly female security guard doing the pat-downs stopped and said, "Look. At. You. Boy!" then started clapping.

Although I was a bit thrown by my dad's insistence that the only way to make a marriage work was to accept that it might not, my anxiety was taking a backseat to my growing excitement as I walked toward my terminal. Asking Amanda to marry me would be one of the biggest, boldest moves of my life—a huge leap for an awkward teen who spent Friday nights watching '80s action movies instead of going to parties, for a Little Leaguer who buried armfuls of porno in his backyard in an insane quest to see his first naked woman. I sucked at girls. I had always sucked at girls. But now I was about to not suck, and it made all the pathetic moments of my past feel like trifles I could laugh at, like bits in a blooper reel at the end of a movie. I couldn't wait to ask her to marry me and take that ring out of the box and slide it on her finger.

What didn't occur to me until I sat down in my aisle seat and we started taxiing down the runway was that I had no idea *how* I was going to ask her. I'd seen the scene in a hundred movies where the guy gets down on one knee, looks his girlfriend in the eye, and proceeds to put into eloquent words all the reasons he loves her and wants her to be his wife. Then she weeps, and they kiss, and her gay male friend says something witty, and her hard-edged sassy female friend who sleeps around breaks down and cries.

I wanted to do something different. But my mind went blank. And stayed that way through the entire hour-and-twenty-minute flight up the California coast. And through the forty-minute subway ride that followed. And after I disembarked and walked through the Mission District, which was bustling with pedestrians, taquerias, and small clothing outlets. And when I realized I had only a few more blocks until I reached the restaurant. My excitement about proposing had become just plain nerves, and all those irrational fears came flooding back.

What if she says no in front of all these people at the restaurant? Why the hell did I want to do this in a crowded place? What if she says no and somebody takes a video of it and puts it on YouTube? Under some title like "Total loser blows proposal." Maybe they wouldn't put "total." That seems egregious. But what if they put bald?! Why am I even worried? There are millions of YouTube videos. No one would ever see it. Maybe I should speak quietly, so they won't be able to get good audio. I've become an insane person. I have to calm down . . .

By the time I stumbled through the large black double doors of Foreign Cinema, sweat was starting to drip down my face, which must have looked particularly alarming since it was a cool fifty degrees outside. A young pale-faced hostess with long black bangs asked, "Can I help you?" the way you ask someone who you hope will turn around and leave.

"Hi. I'm supposed to ask someone to marry me?" I said.

"Uh, okay . . ."

"Sorry—I mean, I have a reservation, I think. Or I should . . ."

"Oh wait, are you Justin?" said a friendlier coworker from behind the bar.

"Yes," I said, wiping the sweat from my brow.

"Come this way," she said. She led me through a crowded outdoor dining area, packed with dozens of customers enjoying eggs benedict, waffles, and bloody marys, and into a plaster-walled room that looked like a miniature art gallery. It was empty, save for one corner where three waiters stood in front of a wooden counter folding napkins and chatting. She grabbed a wooden chair and placed it in the exact center of the empty room, as if it were a piece of art on display.

"Okay, good luck!" she said, then walked away.

I sat down on the chair in the center of the room with the waiters staring at me and looked at my phone. It was 10:20. I noticed that my phone hand was trembling. I knew I was being irrational. This was Amanda, the girl who once told me, "You are my Brad Pitt. And not the weird Brad Pitt when he grew a long beard for some reason." If I could just think of something to say to her, maybe I could calm myself down.

"Okay," I thought, "when she walks in, I'm definitely not gonna get down on one knee and say a bunch of really clichéd things. Amanda hates that stuff as much as I do. I'm just going to walk up to her and tell her exactly how I feel, and how much she means to me, and then ask her if she'll marry me. Then, if she says no, I'll be standing on my own two feet, and I'll be able to walk right out of the restaurant, head held high."

Then I heard voices. I looked up and saw Amanda's friend Madeleine walk into the room, followed by Amanda, who was wearing a lime-green dress that clung to her body. She entered the room, looked right at me, looked away as if she hadn't seen me. "Why can't we just wait for the table by—oh my God!" she said, turning back to me.

All my plans to stay standing were forgotten. I dropped onto one knee, wrestled the ring box from my pocket, and spluttered, "Will you marry me I love you."

"Yes," Amanda said, bursting into tears.

She was still standing about four feet away from me. I got up, approached her, and gave her a kiss. She hugged me and shoved her face into my chest.

"You're really sweaty," she said, laughing as tears streamed down her face.

All the insanity and neuroses that had engulfed my brain washed away. I had a smile so big it seemed impossible, as if I were the guy in an ad for the state lottery and I was holding the winning ticket.

After a minute she finally let go of me, stood up on her tiptoes, and kissed me again. Then I gave her friend Madeleine a hug, as well as the hostess who came to seat us, even though she looked like she didn't necessarily want one.

Before we sat down, Amanda wanted to call her parents, and I decided to call mine as well.

"Hello?" I heard my dad say.

"It's Justin," I said.

"Oh, hey, son. What's happening?"

"I did it," I said.

"You did what?" he asked.

"I proposed to Amanda. She said yes," I replied.

"Well hot damn! Good for you, son. Congratulations. Glad it all worked out. You looked a little nervous this morning. Thought your balls were gonna run up in your asshole for a minute there," he said.

"They almost did."

"Well, good to hear. You now have someone else to drive batshit crazy besides me. Welcome to married life, son."

Acknowledgments

This book would not be possible without the support of so many of my friends. For my friends who appeared in the book, thank you for spending way too much time helping me remember exactly what happened. There's no way I could have filled in all the details without the help of Ryan Walter, Danny Phin, Aaron Estrada, and Jeff Cleator.

Thank you to my father, who read every chapter before anyone else, and let me know when he found things to be "fucking silly." Thank you to my mom and my brothers, Dan, Evan, and Jose, for constantly supporting me throughout the process.

Thanks also to a number of my friends who were always there for me, whether it was to read a draft or just talk through a problem: Cory Jones, Lindsay Goldenberg, Patrick Schumacker, Brian Warner, Brian Huntington, Robert Chafino, Mike Lisbe, Nate Reger, Katie Des Londes, Laura Moran, Brendan Darby, Zack Rosenblatt, Dan Rubin, Lon Zimmet, Robin Shorr, Heather Hicks, Jason Ervin, Casey Phin, Greg Szalay, Scott Satenspiel, George Collins, Chris Von Goetz, and Madeleine Amodeo, and a super-special thank you to Byrd Leavell, who is amazing. Thank you to my editor at HarperCollins, Calvert Morgan, who cleaned up all of my bad habits, and to the rest of the HarperCollins team, Kevin Callahan, Michael Barrs, and Heidi Metcalfe.

Thank you to Kate Hamill, who has been editing every word of this book for the last two years. She is unbelievably talented and tireless, and is responsible for making this book something I could be proud of. I could not have gone through this process without her.

Finally, thank you to my wife, Amanda. She's the best partner I could ever have hoped for, and without her, I wouldn't even have wanted to write this book. Amanda, thank you for letting me drive you insane while I wrote this. Just remember, even when I'm old and decrepit, I'll always bring you a glass of water before bed. I love you.

www.panmacmillan.com